D1130202

# ENGLISH LIT

FROM **JANE AUSTEN** TO **GEORGE ORWELL** AND THE **ENLIGHTENMENT** TO **REALISM,** AN ESSENTIAL GUIDE TO **BRITAIN'S GREATEST WRITERS** AND **WORKS**

# 101

## BRIAN BOONE

Avon, Massachusetts

Published by
Adams Media, a division of F+W Media, Inc.
57 Littlefield Street, Avon, MA 02322. U.S.A.
www.adamsmedia.com

ISBN 10: 1-4405-9971-8
ISBN 13: 978-1-4405-9971-2
eISBN 10: 1-4405-9972-6
eISBN 13: 978-1-4405-9972-9

Printed in the United States of America.

10  9  8  7  6  5  4  3  2  1

Cover design by Michelle Kelly.
Cover images © iStockphoto.com/221A; traveller1116; ClaudioDivizia; borsvelka.

*This book is available at quantity discounts for bulk purchases.*
*For information, please call 1-800-289-0963.*

# DEDICATION

To M.: "I was made and meant to look for you and wait for you and become yours forever." —Robert Browning

# CONTENTS

INTRODUCTION   9

## CHAPTER 1: OLD ENGLISH   11

BEDE'S ECCLESIASTICAL HISTORY
OF THE ENGLISH PEOPLE. . . . . . . . . . . . . . . . . 13

BEOWULF. . . . . . . . . . . . . . . . . . . . . . . . . . 17

THE VISION OF PIERS PLOWMAN . . . . . . . . . . . . 21

WYCLIFFE'S BIBLE. . . . . . . . . . . . . . . . . . . . 25

GEOFFREY CHAUCER. . . . . . . . . . . . . . . . . . . 28

THE KING ARTHUR LEGENDS . . . . . . . . . . . . . . 32

## CHAPTER 2: THE ELIZABETHAN ERA   36

THE KING JAMES BIBLE . . . . . . . . . . . . . . . . . 38

THE BOOK OF COMMON PRAYER . . . . . . . . . . . 43

JOHN DONNE . . . . . . . . . . . . . . . . . . . . . . . 46

CHRISTOPHER MARLOWE. . . . . . . . . . . . . . . . . 50

EDMUND SPENSER . . . . . . . . . . . . . . . . . . . . 54

BEN JONSON . . . . . . . . . . . . . . . . . . . . . . . 58

WILLIAM SHAKESPEARE. . . . . . . . . . . . . . . . . . 62

## CHAPTER 3: THE RESTORATION AND BEYOND   67

JOHN MILTON. . . . . . . . . . . . . . . . . . . . . . . 69

JOHN LOCKE . . . . . . . . . . . . . . . . . . . . . . . 73

DANIEL DEFOE . . . . . . . . . . . . . . . . . . . . . . 78

JONATHAN SWIFT . . . . . . . . . . . . . . . . . . . . . . 82

ALEXANDER POPE. . . . . . . . . . . . . . . . . . . . . . 86

HENRY FIELDING. . . . . . . . . . . . . . . . . . . . . . 90

SAMUEL JOHNSON . . . . . . . . . . . . . . . . . . . . 94

## CHAPTER 4: THE ROMANTIC ERA   99

WILLIAM WORDSWORTH. . . . . . . . . . . . . . . . . .101

SAMUEL TAYLOR COLERIDGE . . . . . . . . . . . . . .103

JANE AUSTEN. . . . . . . . . . . . . . . . . . . . . . . . .107

LORD BYRON . . . . . . . . . . . . . . . . . . . . . . . . .110

WILLIAM BLAKE. . . . . . . . . . . . . . . . . . . . . . . .115

HORACE WALPOLE, MARY SHELLEY, AND GOTHIC
ROMANTICISM . . . . . . . . . . . . . . . . . . . . . . . . .119

ROBERT BURNS . . . . . . . . . . . . . . . . . . . . . . .123

## CHAPTER 5: THE VICTORIAN ERA AND
## THE INDUSTRIAL REVOLUTION   127

ALFRED, LORD TENNYSON . . . . . . . . . . . . . . . .129

CHARLES DICKENS . . . . . . . . . . . . . . . . . . . . .133

GEORGE ELIOT . . . . . . . . . . . . . . . . . . . . . . . .137

THE BRONTË SISTERS . . . . . . . . . . . . . . . . . . .142

ROBERT BROWNING AND
ELIZABETH BARRETT BROWNING . . . . . . . . . . . .148

LEWIS CARROLL . . . . . . . . . . . . . . . . . . . . . . .154

ROBERT LOUIS STEVENSON . . . . . . . . . . . . . . .159

RUDYARD KIPLING. . . . . . . . . . . . . . . . . . . . . .164

OSCAR WILDE. . . . . . . . . . . . . . . . . . . . . . . . .168

THOMAS HARDY . . . . . . . . . . . . . . . . . . . . . . .172

# CHAPTER 6: THE MODERNIST MOVEMENT  176

WILLIAM BUTLER YEATS . . . . . . . . . . . . . . . . . . 177

T.S. ELIOT . . . . . . . . . . . . . . . . . . . . . . . . . 181

D.H. LAWRENCE . . . . . . . . . . . . . . . . . . . . . 187

E.M. FORSTER . . . . . . . . . . . . . . . . . . . . . . . 192

VIRGINIA WOOLF . . . . . . . . . . . . . . . . . . . . . 197

JAMES JOYCE . . . . . . . . . . . . . . . . . . . . . . . 201

W.H. AUDEN . . . . . . . . . . . . . . . . . . . . . . . 207

DYLAN THOMAS . . . . . . . . . . . . . . . . . . . . . 209

# CHAPTER 7: CONTEMPORARY ENGLISH LITERATURE  212

SIR ARTHUR CONAN DOYLE . . . . . . . . . . . . . . 214

GEORGE BERNARD SHAW . . . . . . . . . . . . . . . 218

JOSEPH CONRAD . . . . . . . . . . . . . . . . . . . . . 222

WILLIAM GOLDING . . . . . . . . . . . . . . . . . . . . 227

J.R.R. TOLKIEN AND C.S. LEWIS . . . . . . . . . . . 231

GEORGE ORWELL . . . . . . . . . . . . . . . . . . . . 237

CURRENT VOICES . . . . . . . . . . . . . . . . . . . . 242

**INDEX  248**

# INTRODUCTION

English literature started when there was barely even an English language to use. Dating back a millennium or so, the epic Anglo-Saxon tale of *Beowulf* was the first thing written down in the very earliest version of what would become English. Various Anglo-Saxon groups migrated to the British Isles and brought with them different dialects that would eventually combine to form a single language. It would evolve to become a sophisticated language, and with it would evolve one of the world's most important literary canons: English literature.

Which is to say *British* literature. Literature in the English language is among the most influential and vital in the world, spreading the mechanics of poetry, prose, film, and drama to every corner of the globe. But before there was American literature, or Australian literature, there was the written word of England. And that's what *English Lit 101* is all about. It's a vast, thorough—but simplified and easy to understand—survey of England-based literature.

The authors, poets, and storytellers in the English canon have always tried to answer the big questions: What does it mean to be human? How can rational thought live comfortably with emotions and spirituality? What does it mean to be English?

Uniquely, English authors have approached those big questions by making them personal. Jane Austen's *Pride and Prejudice* may have been about one woman bristling against the confines of society, but it's really just a story about fitting in while being true to oneself. Charles Dickens wrote books that resonated with his Victorian-era audience because they called attention to the social injustices of his day. Personal accounts, whether written in Middle English or delivered in rhythmic verse, reflect universal themes.

In *English Lit 101*, you'll get a glimpse of how major literary forms were created, as well as how they've evolved . . . and amazingly, how they've remained unchanged. (Shakespeare pretty much nailed how a play should be written, and children's authors of today still owe quite a debt to Lewis Carroll, for example.) Here you'll learn how forms change to reflect the prevailing political opinions of their era—such as how poetry went from a way to tell stories and glorify a nation with much pomp and circumstance in the Elizabethan era to the simplified, bare-bones approach befitting the alienation widely felt after World War I. Or how the novel went from showcasing grand tales of adventure (*Robinson Crusoe*) to somber depictions of normal, real life (*Middlemarch*) to getting banned for being *too* real (here's to you, D.H. Lawrence). And through it all, English authors explored, altered, refined, and transformed the English language itself so as to better express the human condition.

English literature is a huge topic that encompasses a lot of material, so here you'll find it broken down by era, and then by each era's major contributors. And with each entry you'll find information on historical context, literary context, and specifically each author's contribution to the canon and why he or she is so important. So whether you're looking to fill in some holes in your knowledge, getting a refresher on what you learned in high school or college, or merely supplementing an English lit course you're taking at this very moment, *English Lit 101* has got you covered.

# Chapter 1

# Old English

To the modern-day reader of contemporary English literature, the earliest examples of "English literature" may seem like they were written in an entirely foreign language ... and they kind of were. The beginnings of the English language took shape in the seventh century after multiple tribes—collectively referred to as Anglo-Saxons—migrated from central Europe to the British Isles. Most spoke Germanic languages—and each tribe spoke its *own* Germanic language—and brought those languages with them. Eventually, those different dialects coalesced into a single language, one with wildly inconsistent spelling and grammar, but a single language nonetheless: Old English.

Old English literature runs concurrent with the Anglo-Saxon era, which comprises works from the seventh century up through to a few decades past the Norman Conquest of 1066. Old English was complex, ever changing, and adaptable. New words and rules became standardized over the centuries, eventually creating a language that was nearly universal across Britain. Language was a necessary tool for communication, and communication became a vital tool for evolving the common tongue.

Very little written material from the Old English era survived, and what documents did survive are primarily what those in power felt was necessary for scribes to record. This is especially true after the large-scale conversion to Christianity by invading Romans. The local church kept records and histories because the monks were the ones who were literate, and many of the Old English documents that we still have around include sermons, church writings translated from Latin, Anglo-Saxon histories, and legal documents. In addition, scribes and poets outside of the sphere of the church's influence wrote down things that weren't quite so dry, things that provide a window into the lives and thoughts of the people who lived in this era. Luckily, those myths, legends, and stories (many of which had been passed down orally for generations) were preserved.

Only about 400 manuscripts total from the Anglo-Saxon period even survive—the expulsion of the Roman-controlled church in the 1500s from England would lead to a lot of intentional document destruction, particularly by way of fire. But these manuscripts would be the basis for a language and a canon that would emerge as comparable, and often superior, to anything ever produced in Greek, Latin, or French.

# BEDE'S ECCLESIASTICAL HISTORY OF THE ENGLISH PEOPLE

The First English Book

Also known as "St. Bede" or "the Venerable Bede," the monk named Bede (672–735) has additionally been called "the father of English history." A historian and archivist at the monastery of Saint Peter in Monkwearmouth in what was at the time the kingdom of Northumbria, Bede was the first to document for the ages the already extensive history of the rapidly growing civilization of the British Isles. To Bede, this history largely meant the rise of Christianity, but this drive to convert the residents of early Britain happened at the same time as the development of the island, as well as the development of what would soon be a common tongue to unite the disparate tribes.

Bede deftly championed English pride as a way to bring about more converts to Christianity by making religious texts more available to Britons. Drawing on his monastery's library of more than 200 volumes of early Catholic Church books, Bede compiled the story of the local church and made it more accessible. His most famous and lasting work is his *Historia ecclesiastica gentis Anglorum* (731). While written in Latin rather than English, this five-book series is the first permanent work to be written in the British Isles. *Ecclesiastical History of the English People*, as it's called in English, was written with the assistance of an abbot named Albinus, and it covers the history of England through the lens of the history of Christianity in Britain. Without Bede's work, which relied on oral histories and interviews in addition to church texts, the details of the Roman invasion and settlement of Britain—really, the history of England itself to that point—would have been lost forever.

# A PEOPLE'S HISTORY

*Historia ecclesiastica* depicts the religious and political history (which are more or less one and the same) of the Anglo-Saxons on the British Isles. This time period runs from the fifth century up to about A.D. 731, which is when Bede finished writing. This book isn't so much literature as it is a methodically delivered historical survey, but this history book makes the history books because it's the oldest text written in England.

## Literary Lessons

One other lasting effect of *Historia ecclesiastica* is that Bede solidified the way the West told time: The books popularized and universalized *anno Domini* as a form of marking years. Prior to this, governments and the church used various local systems, such as *indictions*, which noted the passage of time in fifteen-year cycles, and *regnal years*, a complicated system in which a year was indicated by where it fell inside of a particular monarch's reign.

Any good contemporary literature both reflects its time period and serves as a *de facto* historical document, and *Historia ecclesiastica* certainly qualifies. Bede includes an outline of Roman Britain's geography, reports on significant disagreements between the two main local religious factions (Roman-influenced Christians and Celtic Christians in present-day Ireland and Scotland), and passages on the political uprisings of the 600s, even ones that aren't expressly related to ecclesiastical history. And while books made in England were new, this book's style was not—it was written to emulate the classical history style of the Greeks and Romans.

Bede took his research from those people who historically were the historians and record keepers—monasteries and government records—and he is hardly objective. Less a journalist and more of a storyteller, Bede has a distinct angle and bias: to bring in new Christians. (As Bede later became "St. Bede," that's a telling indication of his aims.) That perspective affected the way he wrote: simply, plainly, and for maximum comprehension.

## MOMENTS IN TIME

Book I of *Historia ecclesiastica* begins in 55 B.C. with the moment Britain became a part of the rest of Europe: when Caesar invaded and brought it into the Roman Empire. The evolution of the Roman Empire into the Holy Roman Empire as it unfolded in Britain is covered, particularly Augustine's A.D. 597 mission to the islands.

Book II concerns the evangelization of Northumbria, which is jeopardized when a pagan king named Penda kills Edwin, the chief missionary.

Book III covers the growth of Christianity under local kings as each is converted to the new religion, and Book IV's main event is the consecration of Theodore, the first to hold the iconic post of the archbishop of Canterbury.

The fifth and final book takes things up to Bede's present day (731), and particularly covers both the conflict between the Roman and British churches over the correct dating of Easter and how

England forged its own identity (in terms of the church) once the Romans departed.

Now a nearly 1,300-year-old document, more than 160 manuscripts of *Historia ecclesiastica* are somehow still intact. That's especially impressive as they were all handwritten and there were probably only ever about 200 copies overall. Bede wrote more than forty more books in his life, mostly biblical commentaries written in Latin, and few of those other manuscripts have survived.

# BEOWULF

A Monster of Early Literature

In 1066, William the Conqueror led troops in the Norman Conquest of England. The new rulers spoke a primitive version of French, which became the official language of the land. Natives of England continued to speak English, which had evolved and combined from related Germanic languages when their Anglo-Saxon and Scandinavian ancestors settled into Britain hundreds of years earlier. *Beowulf* was in that language—Old English—and it survived the reign of French to be recognized as the earliest and oldest surviving work of narrative fiction (literature) in the English language. In fact, it's the first major poem in *any* major latter-day European vernacular, and it's as beautifully written and historically important as anything written by Homer or Virgil.

*Beowulf* is an epic poem, and at 3,182 lines it is the longest in Old English, and one of the longest in any form of English. A classic example (if not *the* classic example, such is its introduction of storytelling tropes) of a hero's journey, the poem tells three simple and straightforward stories. In the first, a monster named Grendel has been terrorizing Heorot, the hall of Geat king Hrothgar (somewhere in present-day Denmark). A prince named Beowulf is called into duty and slaughters Grendel. In the second story, Grendel's mother attempts to avenge her son's death, but she retreats from Beowulf and his army, only for him to follow her to her underwater lair and kill her. The last story flashes forward fifty years, when Beowulf is now king of the Geats. His sins return to haunt him, as now an evil dragon is terrorizing a distant part of his realm. Once more Beowulf goes into battle, defeats the dragon, but is mortally wounded.

## Quotable Voices

"Hwæt we Gar-Dena in gear-dagum
þeod-cyninga, þrym gefrunon,
hu ða æþelingas ellen fremedon."

—from the original text of *Beowulf*


"So. The Spear-Danes in days gone by
and the kings who ruled them had courage and greatness.
We have heard of those princes' heroic campaigns."

—*Beowulf* (Seamus Heaney translation)

# THE CONQUERING HERO

While *Beowulf* takes its material from older, orally passed-down folk tales, it's *Beowulf* that directly gave the English and Western literary canon a lot of the hero mythology and hallmarks of genre fiction still used today. It more or less invented the fantasy genre, although at the time the poem was accepted as just a familiar story, if not one of slightly elevated reality. It's a tale of good versus evil, adventure, destiny, heroism, honor codes, kings, and monsters, and it's divided cleanly into three acts. In these regards, it's quite modern.

*Beowulf* takes place in the sixth century (pinpointed by scholars because of a single reference to a *Beowulf* character mentioned in the works of historian Gregory of Tours), but the story that was solidified and put down on paper by an anonymous poet was composed in the early eleventh century, most likely during the reign of Swedish ruler Cnut the Great (1016–1035). That date was arrived at via analysis of the paper and the scribes' handwriting. That means the actual legend of *Beowulf* was more than 400 years old by the time it was written down, changing as the language of English was created, if not informing the language as it went. At any rate, and even though its characters include monsters, dragons, and mythical kings, the poem does offer insights into a real period of history—Scandinavia, pre A.D. 1000—for which little other knowledge is available.

## THE AGE OF *BEOWULF*

Determining the actual age of the legend *Beowulf* is very tricky. Historians can make parallels from characters to real Scandinavian royalty, for example, and many physical descriptions point its setting to Denmark. Yet it's a relic of early settlements in Britain, suggesting that it's a very old folk tale passed down as an oral tradition to Germanic tribes that settled in Britain; there are similarities and parallels to other Norse, German, and Old English legends. It's an old pagan story, but a Christian poet, who injected Christian motives to the characters, presented it in the written form. Following large-scale conversions of pagan warriors to Christianity at the end of the sixth century, the written *Beowulf* is likely very different from the oral *Beowulf* that was handed down for generations. It's a different beast—the poem is the work of a single poet and is his version of a legend, composed in England as a work of mythology-inspired historical fiction as a way to understand feudal life and Saxon culture.

"It is always better
to avenge dear ones than to indulge in mourning.
For every one of us, living in this world
means waiting for our end. Let whoever can
win glory before death. When a warrior is gone,
that will be his best and only bulwark."

—*Beowulf* (Seamus Heaney translation)

# SURVIVAL AND REVIVAL

Only a single manuscript of the original *Beowulf* has survived, and it's securely housed at the British Library in London. Both the story and the manuscript were forgotten for hundreds of years, and a fire at the library in the 1700s nearly destroyed the copy. In the nineteenth century, linguistics scholars rediscovered the epic, and realized that it played an important role in the early development of the English language, but it wasn't until 1936 that widespread appreciation of *Beowulf* began. This renewed interest was due to Oxford scholar J.R.R. Tolkien. Tolkien gave a speech entitled "*Beowulf*: The Monsters and the Critics," and this speech, later published as a paper, led to recognition of the work as real literature. It was also undeniably an influence on Tolkien's own *The Lord of the Rings*, one of the first modern-day fantasy epics that would go on to influence other fantasy fiction. This means that *Beowulf* uniquely influenced twentieth- and twenty-first-century fiction, but not any other fiction before the twentieth century, despite being 1,000 years old. Because of its obscurity, major British writers like Chaucer and Shakespeare had likely never read *Beowulf*. They probably hadn't even heard of it.

# THE VISION OF PIERS PLOWMAN

It Was All Just a Dream

By the fourteenth century, literature in English beyond religious texts was slowly but surely beginning to emerge. With long poems and simple "mystery" or "morality" plays, English speakers and the purveyors of English literature were moving past using written communication for necessity and direct worship. They were now using it for more personal reasons, such as storytelling. With historical record-keeping and even translations of the Bible in hand, the language had spread and solidified to the point where writers were a bit more free and able to use it to explore what it meant to be human and to express their particular experiences—arguably the two most noble aims of literature. In this regard, *The Vision of Piers Plowman* is among the first, if not *the* first, example of true English literature. And this title is surprisingly complex: Literary historians regard it as the greatest poem in Middle English.

*The Vision of Piers Plowman* (or "*Perys Ploughman*" per the Middle English of the 1360s) is attributed to a poet named William Langland. Little is known of him other than that he wrote the poem, which, accounting for its different permutations, took up the majority of the last twenty years of his life. What is known about Langland was learned from coded references found in *Piers Plowman* itself. It was common for poets of this period to leave clues about themselves in their work, such as acrostic poems that spelled out their names. For Langland, it was a reference to the narrator calling himself "longe wille" and an extremely accurate description of Malvern Hills in the poem's first vision sequence. That range, located in England's West Midlands region, along with the fact that the poem is written in a West Midlands dialect, means Langland was probably from the West Midlands.

# VISIONS AND SYMBOLS

The text itself is not a simple story at all, and it was written long before distinct genres of narrative formed, which means the poem is difficult to categorize. It's best described as an allegorical tale about a man named Will—a regular person (not a noble or royalty) and audience surrogate meant to represent all of humanity—who is inadvertently thrust into a quest for salvation and meaning via a series of visions. The events of the poem unfold only after Will goes to sleep and he escapes into the world of dreams and the exploration of his soul, where the concepts of the universe and faith are rendered as real objects and living figures. For example, Will sees a tower where "Truth" dwells, a deep dungeon of sadness, and in between them a "field full of folk" where all of humanity demonstrate their various trades.

In the field, Will meets a plowman named Piers (a stand-in for Christ) who helps him envision a doomed world undone by human frailty. Will contemplates how man can both live in the world but also be spiritually above the world. *Piers Plowman* is one of the first philosophical texts in the English language, and is also an early exploration of allegory and the nature of a protagonist. It's narrative fiction, but one that appeals to its audience on a very simple but deep level.

Despite the religious themes and intent of this work, it's highly critical of the Catholic Church, taking particular aim at corrupt priests. Because of that, the text inspired the English movement that demanded local control of the church, instead of control from the Catholic Church leaders who were stationed far away in Rome. Less than 200 years later, that movement would culminate with King Henry VIII eliminating the Catholic Church as the state religion in favor of the newly formed Church of England.

# ALLITERATION AND ILLUSTRATION

While it's defined as a poem, *Plowman* does not employ the rigid structure that defines most forms of poetry. It's divided into two main parts (Vision 1 and Vision 2) that are then broken down into seven sections or *passus* (Latin for "steps") that vary in length from 129 to 642 lines. A particular rhyme scheme isn't used, but the poem is written in a form of alliterative poetry dating to the Anglo-Saxon period. It derives a kind of rhythm from the repetition of consonant sounds. Thanks to *Plowman,* this format would become commonly used by writers, notably in works like *Sir Gawain and the Green Knight* and *Le Morte d'Arthur*, the first major English-language collection of the King Arthur legends (which are discussed later in this chapter).

Also unique about *Plowman* is that there isn't one definitive manuscript of it, even though it's attributable to a single writer. Three distinct versions of the poem have survived, which scholars have labeled "A," "B," and "C." Here's how they break down:

- The A text is 2,567 lines with two visions and seven passus, and Langland wrote it between 1367 and 1370.
- The B text is an extensive rewrite and extension of the A text, totaling 7,277 lines with eight visions and a total of twenty passus, dating to 1377.
- The C text has twenty-two passus and was created in 1385 when Langland revised the B text. Langland likely revised the C after leaders of the Peasants' Revolt of 1381 cited *Piers Plowman* as an inspiration; the C is decidedly less political (or anti-Catholic) and more personal than the B text.

*Piers Plowman* remained popular well into the sixteenth century as a Protestant text, as it promotes a personal relationship with Christ and downplays the need for the hierarchy of organized religion. It's also a step to real English literature in that it tries to explain the concepts of what it means to be human via storytelling and symbolism. It's an early example of a writer making his own experiences into art, which would serve as the groundwork for the romantic era a mere 400 years in the future.

# WYCLIFFE'S BIBLE

Now Available in English

When John Wycliffe's translation of the Bible, known as Wycliffe's Bible, first emerged in 1382, many English Christians finally got what they wanted—a Bible in their own vernacular. Being able to read and/or understand when read aloud (the majority of Britons were illiterate) the finer points of their religion led many to question the Catholic Church's authority as well as the received dogma. This questioning of how the Catholic Church operated, encouraged by Wycliffe's translation of the Bible, laid the seeds of the Reformation: the major event of the sixteenth century in which Britain broke away from the Catholic Church and established the Church of England.

## A BUILDING RESENTMENT

John Wycliffe was born in Yorkshire in 1320, a time in which the Roman Catholic Church held total power over Christianity and its adherents in England (in tension with the Crown, which had absolute power over matters of state). Wycliffe attended Oxford for biblical studies, and while there he pored over the scriptures. He began to notice that some of the things the church was advocating (and claiming biblical support for) did not match up with the actual holy text. This inspired Wycliffe to study the Latin Bible that much harder to find more discrepancies, and as he found more inconsistencies his resentment for the mother church grew.

But at least Wycliffe knew Latin—the average person in England didn't. He figured that if the Bible were available in English,

Christians in England would be interested to learn more about their religion in their own language. And even if a regular person *did* know Latin, it was still quite difficult to obtain scriptures for study. Wycliffe lived in the pre–printing press era, so only hand-transcribed manuscripts were available, and even those were only available to those credentialed at Oxford or Cambridge.

## GIVE THE PEOPLE WHAT THEY WANT

From 1348 to 1350, the Black Death killed around a third of all Europeans. Bad things were happening, people felt subhuman and betrayed by God, and they wanted answers that they couldn't get from a mass delivered in Latin. That motivated Wycliffe more than ever to provide a Bible that regular people could read. Appointed a master in 1361 at one of the colleges that made up Oxford, he started to work on translating the Latin Bible into English. He collaborated with as many as three assistants, but he translated a great deal himself, including all four Gospels and most of the rest of the New Testament. After more than twenty years, Wycliffe's English Bible was complete and was being hand-copied by scribes for mass distribution by 1382. Wycliffe passed away in 1384, but his chief assistant, John Purvey, headed up revisions in 1388 and 1395.

The English Bible was troubling not only to the Crown but to Rome, as the church was not happy to have its authority threatened or to find that the English were altering scripture to suit their own ends. In 1401, Henry IV and Parliament passed the *De heretico comburendo* ("on the burning of heretics") laws that allowed the state to burn at the stake anyone found guilty of heresy (going against the church's established beliefs). Though the statutes didn't mention

Wycliffe, they were firmly aimed at him and his followers (known as Lollards). At the Third Synod of Oxford in 1408, the Catholic Church declared that the Bible couldn't be translated into English without the church's approval, which it would likely not provide. Then, at the Council of Constance, in 1415, church leaders declared John Wycliffe, who had been dead for thirty-one years, a *heretic*, someone whose ideas were considered dangerously out of line with those of the Catholic Church. They ordered that all of his works—*all* of his papers, not just copies of Wycliffe's Bible—were to be burned. The Council also passed a ruling that said that anyone in England who so much as read an English Bible:

"would forfeit land, cattle, life and goods from their heirs forever."

Finally, in 1428, church officials exhumed Wycliffe's corpse, burned it, and threw his ashes in a river.

Fortunately, Wycliffe's supporters had received enough advance notice after the rulings of the Council of Constance in 1415 to start saving as many handwritten manuscripts as they could before they were confiscated and destroyed. Around 250 survived...along with the seeds of the Reformation.

## Quotable Voices

"Dominus regit me, et nihil mihi deerit."

—Psalm 23 in the Latin Vulgate

"The Lord gouerneth me, and no thing schal faile to me."

—Psalm 23 in Wycliffe's Bible

# GEOFFREY CHAUCER

The Birth of English Poetry

By the end of the fourteenth century, England was a united nation with a united language. English became the official language of the country in 1362, and by 1386 it had replaced French as the language used in schools. It was universal, accepted, and had been mastered by enough people that it could move from a tool of communication to one of art and storytelling. The time was ripe for new poets and writers to embrace the language, and no one did this better than Geoffrey Chaucer (1340–1400).

Chaucer lived a varied life, working as a solider, valet, clerk, and finally a high-ranking diplomat, which afforded him the chance to travel throughout Europe. All the while, he was collecting characters and observing human behavior to inform his writing. Chaucer was called "the Father of English Literature" and is also regarded as the greatest poet of the Middle Ages. More specifically, Chaucer is the father of English poetry, and the creator of English *narrative poetry*— poems that tell a story from beginning to end.

## Literary Lessons

In 1360, during the Hundred Years' War, Chaucer was kidnapped in France, and King Edward III paid the modern equivalent of a few hundred thousand dollars for his safe return.

Chaucer also displaced the Anglo-Saxon alliterative method and introduced the *heroic couplet*, which involves meter, rhyme schemes, and accented syllables: all structural hallmarks of poetry that would dictate the form for centuries. A line of verse in this style has ten syllables, in which every other syllable is accented; each set of two lines rhymes at the end.

## THE CANTERBURY TALES

Geoffrey Chaucer's masterwork, written between 1387 and 1400, is *The Canterbury Tales*. It's a series of incredibly varied story poems told by a variety of people from many different walks of life and social positions, each of which subtly showcases the diversity found in medieval England. The overall premise of *The Canterbury Tales* is that thirty travelers—strangers, mostly—meet at an inn outside of London on the eve of a 60-mile pilgrimage to Canterbury to visit the shrine of St. Thomas Becket. That pilgrimage was a common ritual of the day, and was deeply meaningful to some of the travelers, but most are just there to have a good time. The innkeeper suggests that they all tell stories along the way to Canterbury—each person gets to tell two on the way and two on the way back. Whoever tells the best one, according to the innkeeper, gets a free dinner at the conclusion of the trip.

This setup was the first poetry collection in English literature, and really, the first short-story anthology. Moreover, that structure allowed Chaucer the freedom to tell lots of seemingly unrelated stories, especially as the different pilgrims react to each other's tales, creating a cohesive whole out of the various tales.

Each tale is identified by the pilgrim who tells it. "The Knight's Tale" is probably the most famous in *The Canterbury Tales*, because it involves knights and a love triangle. Drawing the shortest straw and the opportunity to go first, the Knight delivers an epic romantic tale about two knights who spend years competing for the same woman's love. Next is "The Miller's Tale," which is about an old carpenter being cheated on by his young wife. (This tale prompts the very angry Reeve—a low-ranking politician, and a former carpenter—to tell his own story, "The Reeve's Tale," a derogatory story about another miller.) The Cook, the Man of Law, the Monk, the Prioress, and many more all get a turn. Chaucer actually never finished the book—he only got one-fifth of the way through before he died in 1400. But the scope of the work, and its variety, is remarkable. There are tales of romance, trickery, adultery, myth, fairy tales, sermons, stories of saints, allegory, and even parody. All are presented with as much emotional sensitivity and realism as Chaucer's characters. The stories are about real people with feelings, emotions, complexities, and contradictions.

## Quotable Voices

"But for to telle yow al hir beautee,
It lyth nat in my tonge, n'yn my konnyng;
I dar nat undertake so heigh a thyng.
Myn Englissh eek is insufficient.
It moste been a rethor excellent
That koude his colours longynge for that art,
If he sholde hire discryven every part.
I am noon swich, I moot speke as I kan."

—*The Canterbury Tales*

# STORIES IN POEM FORM

While the Middle English language that *The Canterbury Tales* was written in may seem stilted today, this is only because the language kept evolving. And even though these stories were written in the very specific heroic couplet style, Chaucer's language is the vernacular of the day; poetic structure combined with common speech. These stories (or poems) are effective because Chaucer chose to write them in the way people really talked at the time—because they are stories about all kinds of aspects of regular life, told by regular people. And the poet writes them in the way each individual speaks, according to class and character, making for a tapestry of rich characters who are all unique. Had he written in the established literary languages of Latin or French, *The Canterbury Tales* would not have been a very effective work, and readers at the time may not have connected so strongly with it.

These stories were written for normal people that regular readers (or those being read to) could understand and relate to. Good literature not only describes the human experience, but it *relates* the human experience. Chaucer was among the first English writers to realize that. Along with that realism, Chaucer lent his work an energy and vitality—and a raunchiness—that was (and still is) rarely seen in poetry, and certainly not in the mostly religion-oriented English literature that preceded him.

# THE KING ARTHUR LEGENDS

All Hail the King

The King Arthur tales are among the most definitively "English" works of the English canon. The stories of Arthur, Lancelot, Excalibur, Guinevere, the Knights of the Round Table, Merlin, the Lady of the Lake, Avalon, and all the other elements of the Arthurian sagas have captivated generations with their tales of honor, romance, and adventure, and they have remained remarkably unaltered over the centuries. While they provide historical context for what England may have been like in the Dark and Middle Ages, they aren't *exactly* true (unfortunately, magic swords aren't real). And they aren't even completely *English*—the stories originated in France and Wales.

## A WELSH TALE

The Arthurian legends have been traced back as far as the ninth century, in Wales, when a monk named Nennius wrote a history of a warlord named Arthur who was said to have led the Britons into a dozen battles against Saxon invaders in the sixth century, including the Battle of Mount Badon in 518. (However, the historian Gildas wrote about the real Battle of Mount Badon in 518 as it happened, and he made no mention of a military general named Arthur.) Historians agree that King Arthur was a literary figure, a mishmash of mythological figures and tribal warlords from Celtic Britain. *Historia Regum Britanniae* (*The History of the Kings of Britain*), written by Geoffrey of Monmouth in 1132, collects some of the King Arthur stories but incorrectly presents them as factual.

## Quotable Voices

"Then sir Bedwere cryed and seyd,
'A, my lorde Arthur, what shall becom of me, now ye go frome me and leve me here alone amonge myne enemyes?'
'Comforte thyselff,' seyde the kynge, 'and do as well as thou mayste, for in me ys no truste for to truste in.'"

—*Le Morte d'Arthur*

The Arthurian tales as we now know them were collected, translated, and written down by Thomas Malory. Malory was the lord of a country manor when, in 1450, for reasons not quite understood, he became a bloodthirsty criminal almost overnight. Along with some cohorts, more akin to a small army, he threatened to murder a duke and then ransacked an abbey (among other crimes). Malory spent most of the decade in London's Newgate Prison (without a trial), and to pass the time he decided to write. An educated lord, he was the rare literate prisoner at the time, and he figured it would occupy his mind and his time if he collected and put into English what he later recollected as "the whole book of King Arthur and his noble knights of the Round Table."

But the written tales as Malory had known them were from a narrative French poem from the late 1300s, adapted from the Welsh folk tales by way of *Historia Regum Britanniae*. He sought to translate the French stories into English, while also adapting them for a fifteenth-century English audience, embellishing and Anglicizing the story wherever he could. Among the events of the twenty-one books of story in verse that Malory produced, you'll find stories about:

- the founding of King Arthur's kingdom
- the creation of the Round Table
- the quest for the Holy Grail
- the fall of Arthur's kingdom
- the death of King Arthur to a mortal wound
- Arthur's request to have his mighty sword Excalibur returned to its place of origin, with the Lady of the Lake

## KING ARTHUR, ENGLISH ICON

The other half of the duo that made King Arthur iconic was printer William Caxton. One of the first mass printers in Britain, he produced and translated more than 100 books and pamphlets, for which he wrote his own prefaces and epilogues. These sections were instructional and gave his books authority by adding literary criticisms, first-person thoughts and feelings, and more information that told readers exactly why what they were reading was important. Caxton was a champion of British writing (among his other printings: *The Canterbury Tales*), and he stabilized, standardized, and cleaned up a lot of the still developing English language, particularly spelling and grammar, so as to make it easier to learn (and read—it was good for business for English to be easy).

Caxton published Malory's product in 1484 in English under the French title *Le Morte d'Arthur* (or "The Death of Arthur," which is how it ends). Also culturally impactful was a companion title that Caxton released around the same time called *The Book of the Order of Chivalry*. Recalling a distant, if nonexistent "simpler" time, *The Book of the Order of Chivalry* pointed out to readers that the King Arthur legends demonstrated how men were men, but that all people were decent—even though the book was fiction, and even though Malory had written it while in prison for violent crimes. Malory's time was one of upheaval, and *The Book of the Order of Chivalry* reignited interest in aristocratic values, such as loyalty and peace, that had been lost due to the Wars of the Roses (on-and-off conflicts spanning from 1455 to 1487 between rival factions for control of the English throne).

## NATIONAL TREASURE

The mythology of *Le Morte d'Arthur* and the lessons of *The Book of the Order of Chivalry* spoke to the masses, and both were highly successful. And since the printing press had been invented several decades prior, thousands were able to actually read them.

*Le Morte d'Arthur* captured both the imagination and national pride of the people. And through the virtue of language ownership, it pushed a solidification of English as the unifying language of Great Britain. Almost as importantly, *Le Morte d'Arthur* marks the birth of British popular fiction and entertainment. There was no need for these books; they served no specific political or ecclesiastical purpose. They were just *fun*.

# Chapter 2

# The Elizabethan Era

Also known as the English Renaissance, the Elizabethan era was the golden age of English literature. This time period, which ran approximately from 1558 to 1603, was an unparalleled era of growth and quality of the written word, characterized by the development of the novel, new and lasting innovations in poetry, and new styles of theater that would incubate the most important and popular plays in the English language.

While Queen Elizabeth I, the monarch of the time, didn't directly affect the art of the day, the tone of her reign was one of English pride, prosperity, and political dominance. The English were thriving, not merely surviving, and life was comfortable enough that writing was a viable trade, not just a pursuit afforded to those from wealthy families. (Theater was still viewed as a low art for commoners, but William Shakespeare and Ben Jonson would dispel that notion.)

The Elizabethan era was a great leap forward after the experimentation and baby steps of the previous 500 years, in which literature was primarily a tool for politics and religion. Writers now explored a variety of topics, especially any and all aspects of the human condition. But despite that commitment to realism, works were not presented in an entirely realistic way. Poems and theater of this era were especially noted for their flowery, emotional speech and were driven by meter and a rhyme scheme that was well suited to performance.

Celebrating the language was a form of national pride—important as England circumnavigated and conquered the globe, spreading "Englishness" throughout. With this exploration and contact with other cultures came new words from foreign languages that writers were eager to add to their toolboxes. By doing so, these writers helped make English a vaster and more expressive language.

This exploration of the globe, and the trade that came with it, meant more prosperity, which led to a growing middle class and increased literacy (and the solidification of the rules of English). This emerging and increasingly sophisticated audience now had the time and money for entertainment.

# THE KING JAMES BIBLE

A Transformative Translation

As you know, the work commonly referred to as the "King James Bible" is not the first book in the English language. Nor is it even the first Bible in English, and not even the first English-language Bible produced in England. It is, however, the first mass-printed book in English. What makes the King James Bible stand out among other English Bibles is that it's literature—the team who wrote it went far and above the assigned task of translation and made it a beautiful work of art.

While Wycliffe's Bible was a watershed moment in the history of English, it had its flaws and its detractors. It was a solid translation that brought the Bible to English readers, but politically it was a relic of another time. After the Reformation and the creation of the Church of England, anti-Catholic sentiment was so rampant in Britain that Wycliffe's Bible fell out of favor. It was seen as a Catholic Bible, and thus unfit for a Protestant nation. The leaders of the Church of England were subsequently more critical of the text itself, convinced there were inaccuracies as it had been translated from Latin, and not the Greek and Hebrew in which it was originally written. In other words, Wycliffe's Bible was a translation of a translation. England had grown too sophisticated, and too Protestant, and needed a new Bible that did away with the Catholic Church's influence entirely: England needed a direct translation from the ancient languages into common English.

# BUILDING A BETTER BIBLE

There had been a few attempts at a more accurate English Bible, even before the Reformation. William Tyndale, an English contemporary of the Protestant reformer Martin Luther (the German minister who led the Lutheran Church, the first group to successfully break away from the Catholic Church), translated the New Testament directly into English in 1525, and then did the same to the Old Testament in 1535. For his efforts, the Catholic Church rewarded him with an execution on charges of heresy. Tyndale's Bible was revised and became the Great Bible of 1539, which was the Church of England's first Bible, sanctioned by Henry VIII himself when he authorized a clean and total split from Rome.

## Literary Lessons

The Church of England not meeting their demands ultimately led the Puritans to depart for America. While the religious group led by William Bradford supported the idea of England's split from the Catholic Church, they didn't like the end result of the split—the rituals of mass were still too similar to the Catholic mass for their tastes. So, the Puritans (of which the root word is "pure") started forming their own churches with their own rules and rituals, which was viewed as treason by the Church of England. Because of this, Puritans were widely attacked, and this violence led so many to the wilds of New England.

Still, the book was seen as lackluster and not the effective tool or beautiful translation that church leaders wanted or needed their holy text to be. After his coronation in 1603, King James convened the Hampton Court Conference in January 1604 to meet with Church of England leaders. The group decided that a new English-language Bible reflecting the nation's unique, non-Catholic needs was necessary. The members of the ultraconservative Puritan faction were especially in favor, as they found previous English translations entirely unsuitable. For example, there were two errors in the Great Bible—typos, really—that Puritan leaders said called the whole translation into question:

- In Psalm 28, "They were not obedient" is a translation of "They were not disobedient."
- In Psalm 30, "Then stood up Phinees and prayed" left out the key phrase "executed judgment."

The main decision handed down by the Hampton Court Conference was that the new translation had to be not only accurate to the original texts, but more importantly, familiar and understandable to both readers and listeners (as most commoners in England were illiterate and would just be hearing the passages recited in church services) alike. King James asked the scribes to use another early English Bible, the Bishops' Bible (produced in 1568), as a guide and told them to especially retain that book's spelling of biblical names.

Forty-seven scholars, all of them members of the Church of England, worked for seven years on the new Bible, translating it directly from the original texts. The staff was broken down into smaller groups who worked on individual sections separately and then compared them to the work of the other committees to account for a similar tone. None of these scholars were paid, but they were guaranteed royal patronage (an annual fee paid out by the government) and positions at churches and colleges when they finished. Ultimately, their work comprised thirty-nine Old Testament books, twenty-seven New Testament books, and fifteen other books of Apocrypha, which have been left out of later editions of the Bible after church scholars judged them to be inauthentic.

## Literary Lessons

The common phrases introduced into English after appearing in the King James Bible include: "the blind leading the blind," "the writing is on the wall," "there's nothing new under the sun," "a drop in the bucket," "can a leopard change its spots," "broken heart," "sign of the times," "powers that be," "rise and shine," "how the mighty have fallen," "nothing but skin and bones," and "eat, drink, and be merry."

# THE GOOD BOOK

Robert Barker was the king's official printer (and his dad had been the printer for Elizabeth I) and was tasked with printing the first edition of the King James Bible in 1611. King James had asked for a workable Bible for his subjects and the Church of England, and he got that, but he also got a work of art and a landmark in English-language literature. The King James Version of the Bible is both scholarly and direct, and written with a poetic flair and masterful command of the English language. It was written by a committee of forty-seven, yet reads like it's the work of a single author.

By 1700, the King James Bible was the unchallenged English Bible in the Church of England, alongside *The Book of Common Prayer*, which is discussed in the following entry. Ironically, the Bible that had been created to confirm the split from the Catholic Church has been adopted as the Bible for English-speaking Catholics worldwide. By 1900, it was the most widely printed book in history—or at least the revision of 1769 by Oxford scholars was, which omitted the Apocrypha.

## Literary Lessons

The name of the King James Bible on the first edition's title page was "THE HOLY BIBLE, Containing the Old Testament, AND THE NEW: Newly Translated out of the Original tongues: & with the former Translations diligently compared and revised, by his Majesties special Commandment." By 1814, it was commonly referred to as the "King James Bible" or "King James Version."

# THE BOOK OF COMMON PRAYER

Uncommonly Original

Also known as the *Anglican Book of Prayer*, *The Book of Common Prayer* is the official prayer book of the Church of England. It's the step-by-step guide to the church service, along with explanation and commentary. It's really a series of books, because it was revised several times from its first issuing in 1549 until it was finalized in 1662. Remarkably, *The Book of Common Prayer* was a part of Anglican services, mostly unchanged, all the way until 1980. Written in the rich, poetic style indicative of the Elizabethan era in which it was created, it was also the basis for the prayer books and worship guides for other European Protestant religions of the same vintage, such as Methodism and Lutheranism.

Being the official book of the official state religion of England meant that *The Book of Common Prayer* would be the first, if not only, book many English would read besides the Bible. Almost an entire nation was exposed to this book and its still new national language, the language of the burgeoning British Empire. It remains one of the most widely distributed and read books in history.

## BY OFFICIAL DECREE

Thomas Cranmer was the archbishop of Canterbury from 1533 to 1555, overlapping the rulership of three different monarchs. While the reigning monarch of England is technically the figurehead of the Church of England, the archbishop of Canterbury is the day-to-day leader of the religious organization. During the rule of King Edward

VI (1547–1553), Cranmer sought to provide the English with a liturgy that was in English, so as to seal the split from the Roman Catholic Church, which dictated that all masses be held in Latin (and which had historically executed religious leaders in England who had tried otherwise).

The format of *The Book of Common Prayer* follows the calendar year, providing a framework for weekly church services along with special observances for Lent, Holy Week, and the Christmas season. It's based on Catholic mass guidelines, as Cranmer didn't want to create anything too different than what congregants were used to. But he was committed to the *English* church, so his main directive was to create a liturgy that was in readily understandable, plain English. To establish the English church as something apart from Catholicism, Cranmer introduced some significant changes. For example, saints are presented as good Christian role models, as opposed to their role in Catholicism as supernatural figures or *intercessors*: those who can pray on one's behalf. When it was issued in 1549, *The Book of Common Prayer* marked the first time that complete church services along with liturgies for daily masses and sacraments such as baptism, confirmation, prayers for the sick, and marriage were available in English.

## FOLLOWING ALONG

Cranmer's first edition of *The Book of Common Prayer*, which he edited, compiled, and translated (with the assistance of other religious leaders and scholars), was issued in 1549. An act of Parliament made it the official liturgy of the English church. Nevertheless, response was lackluster—conservative groups such as the Puritans found it to be too much of a shift from the Catholic mass, and liberal groups thought it was too similar to the Catholic mass. Cranmer dutifully revised the book, and a second edition was issued in 1552. Cranmer and his successors continued to field input from church leaders (and factions) over the decades, and minor changes resulted in new editions of *The Book of Common Prayer* that were issued during the reigns of Elizabeth I and James I. The 1662 edition, in use for more than 300 years, was still almost entirely the work of Cranmer and his staff. Alternate services were published as an addendum to the book in 1980, all in an attempt, like the original, at helping congregants understand the belief system of their church with clear, direct language.

## Literary Lessons

Because the various permutations of *The Book of Common Prayer* were so widely read and distributed, it's not surprising that turns of phrase that Cranmer and his associates created for the book would make their way into common use. What is surprising is how good those phrases were, proving that Cranmer succeeded in writing in and for the common vernacular. Among those phrases: "ashes to ashes, dust to dust," "peace in our time," and "'til death do us part." That last one comes from the book's instructions for wedding services, which have become the Western standard, regardless of denomination.

# JOHN DONNE

Metaphysical Poetry

While earlier English poetry certainly discussed spiritual themes (not to mention nationalistic ones), it was always firmly and specifically within the realm of Christianity—man's relationship to the Judeo-Christian God of the Bible and an application of biblical concepts to regular life. But, by the early seventeenth century, the English language and English philosophy had advanced to the point where a deeply thoughtful and critical writer like John Donne was both possible and necessary.

## Quotable Voices

> "Death, be not proud, though some have called thee
> Mighty and dreadful, for thou art not so;
> For those whom thou think'st thou dost overthrow
> Die not, poor Death, nor yet canst thou kill me."
>
> —"Holy Sonnet 10"

Born into a Catholic family in 1572 at a time of heavy Catholic persecution in England, Donne attended but did not graduate from Oxford because he wouldn't convert to the Church of England. He eventually gave in, which greatly informed the poetry of a man who was forever conflicted and curious about his faith.

Donne's poetry elevated English poetry to new and complex intellectual heights. His work went beyond Christianity and questioned and examined the very nature of spirituality itself, particularly the constant conflict between what Donne called the "sacred and pro-fane," meaning things that are holy and things that are ordinary. Donne's work is indicative of the broad English cultural and political theme of his time: wild exploration and experimentation (at least in the mind or on paper).

# EARLY WORKS

Donne studied law and was headed for a career as a diplomat, but instead spent the 1590s blowing an inheritance from his late father on books, travel, and wooing women, upon whom he honed his craft by writing erotic poems. His works *Satyres* and *Songs and Sonnets* were published in small print runs, and he built up a small but devoted fol-lowing. He got serious—and serious about writing—in 1593, after his brother was convicted of "Catholic sympathies" and died in prison. Donne questioned his faith, and as stated earlier, joined the Church of England. Shortly thereafter he found work as the private secretary to Sir Thomas Egerton, Lord Keeper of the Great Seal of England.

In 1601, he secretly married his boss's sixteen-year-old niece, Anne More (a descendent of Sir Thomas More), a wedding of which More's family did not approve. More's father had Donne thrown in prison, but he was released shortly after he proved the marriage was valid.

In 1610, Donne renounced his Catholic faith officially with an essay called "Pseudo-Martyr," arguing that Catholics could support the English monarchy without compromising their religious loyalty to Rome. Back in good graces with the government and the church, he wrote prose examining religious ideas and worked his way up through the hierarchy and was named the dean of St. Paul's, for St.

Paul's Cathedral in London, in 1621. After his wife died and he himself faced severe illness, Donne wrote a prayer book called *Devotions upon Emergent Occasions*, which unsurprisingly dealt primarily with Donne's palpable fear of death.

## Quotable Voices

"No man is an island, entire of itself;
every man is a piece of the continent, a part of the main."

—"Meditation XVII," *Devotions upon Emergent Occasions*

All the while, Donne produced volumes of poetry. Along with George Herbert, Richard Crenshaw, and Henry Vaughan, Donne was the first in a group of poets that Samuel Johnson, writing in the eighteenth century, would call the "metaphysical poets." This style of poetry in general, and Donne's in particular, didn't soothe the reader, or try to make sense of the world through pastoral description or other common poetic techniques. Instead, he startled and unsettled readers in order to get them to think about the big truths that poets are forever grappling with: the meaning of life, the nature of love, mankind's place in the universe, etc. He did this by presenting paradoxes, contradictory images, wordplay, bizarre imagery, and by including little-known references to art and religion.

# THE CONCEIT

Donne's greatest and most definitive contribution to poetry is the metaphysical conceit. A *conceit* is an extended metaphor (meaning it runs through the entire poem) that compares two concepts or objects that one wouldn't normally think would go together. A metaphysical conceit does the same but uses even more out-there associations, connecting sensory observations with abstract principles.

Because there isn't an obvious link between the objects being compared, the reader is forced to find similarities between them, while also being well aware of how dissimilar they are. In Donne's "A Valediction: Forbidding Mourning," a couple about to be separated is compared, however oddly, to a compass:

"If they be two, they are two so / As stiff twin compasses are two; / Thy soul, the fixed foot, makes no show / To move, but doth, if the other do."

The couple's spiritual connection works like a compass: One is anchored in the center while the other circles around it. And in the concluding lines ("Thy firmness makes my circle just, / And makes me end where I begun"), the one in the center helps to complete the one circling.

And then there's "The Flea." It's a poem of seduction, in which the narrator tries to romance a lady, but he does so in an incredibly roundabout manner. He points out that they've both been bitten by the same flea and describes how titilating it is that their blood is mixing together inside the stomach of the parasitic bug:

"Yet this enjoys before it woo, / And pampered swells with one blood made of two, / And this, alas, is more than we would do."

How romantic.

# CHRISTOPHER MARLOWE

Drawing a Blank

Christopher Marlowe was born in 1564, the son of a Canterbury shoemaker, but before long he was well on his way to a career as a scholar and writer while studying at Cambridge. Classically trained and aiming to write in the classical style, Marlowe wrote some narrative poetry and translated the works of Ovid, but then his life took a left turn … and then a few more. Evidence from the time suggests he took several trips to Europe as a spy, which says nothing of the things that actually wound up on his rap sheet.

In 1589, he was involved in a street fight in which another poet killed a man. In 1592, he was deported from the Netherlands when he was caught trying to sell forged gold coins. And in 1593, he got into a fight with a businessman named Ingram Frizer in a Deptford tavern over the bill—and Frizer killed Marlowe. He was just twenty-nine when he died, but despite the criminal activity and his young age, he'd already built up a reputation as one of the most innovative and important playwrights of his era.

Marlowe primarily wrote histories and tragedies for a theater group called the Admiral's Men, including *The Tragedie of Dido, Queene of Carthage*; *The Jew of Malta*; and the smash hit *Tamburlaine the Great*. With *Tamburlaine*, Marlowe revived the unpopular form of the theatrical tragedy, which had been out of favor on the English stage for decades.

## CREATING BLANK VERSE

Just before he died, Marlowe published his most famous play, *The Tragical History of the Life and Death of Doctor Faustus*, which he had slowly worked on for most of the 1590s. The play wouldn't be performed until 1604, but the published version in 1594 sold briskly. With this play, Marlowe popularized a style called *blank verse*, which is nonrhyming poetic verse. Invented by an obscure sonnet writer named Henry Surrey in the 1540s, blank verse is delivered in *iambic pentameter*. That means a line consists of ten syllables with five feet, or alternating stressed and unstressed syllables, or nonrhyming heroic couplets. Rhyme doesn't necessarily make words into poetry—structure and meter do (at least as far as this era of English poetry is concerned)—and Marlowe made this structure and meter his own.

Based on a Greek form called *iambic trimeter* that used twelve-syllable lines with six emphasized syllables, Surrey and Marlowe knew that English was a slower-moving, tighter language than Greek, and having fewer syllables in a line would make for a more poetic, flowing, and less stilted dialogue. Marlowe's blank verse gave writers newfound creative freedom while still operating within a structure. Blank verse became the standard for how English drama (as well as epic poetry) would be presented in the Elizabethan era.

## THE FAUSTIAN BARGAIN

The plot and themes of *Doctor Faustus* are as important to literature as the way in which Marlowe wrote its lines of dialogue. The play is based on the medieval legend of a magician who summons Mephistopheles, a demon and loyal servant of Satan, to whom he sells his soul in exchange for fame and fortune. The Faust story was enjoying a resurgence in popularity in Europe in the sixteenth century after the story had been published in German for the first time and then translated into English. Marlowe's theatrical version marks the first dramatization of the story in any language. In the original legend, Faustus is a magician; in Marlowe's he's a more relatable (and familiarly frightening) bored scientist, hungry for power and adventure. Dr. Faustus subsequently trades his soul in return for twenty-four years of Mephistopheles acting as his personal genie, granting all of his wishes and whims, which primarily amount to frivolities and practical jokes. A standout scene is an underwhelming meeting with Helen of Troy. This spawned the familiar quote:

"Was this the face that launched a thousand ships?"

The most poignant scene in *Doctor Faustus* is the final one, in which the doctor dies and realizes that he's on his way to a very bad place and that he's completely wasted his life.

## Quotable Voices

"Ah, Faustus.
Now hast thou but one bare hour to live,
And then thou must be damn'd perpetually!
Stand still, you ever-moving spheres of heaven,
That time may cease, and midnight never come;
Fair Nature's eye, rise, rise again, and make
Perpetual day; or let this hour be but
A year, a month, a week, a natural day,
That Faustus may repent and save his soul!"

—*The Tragical History of the Life and Death of Doctor Faustus*

While Marlowe's life and career were cut extremely short, he was highly admired and extremely influential among future writers as well as contemporaries. Playwright George Peele eulogized him as "Marley, the Muses darling." Ben Jonson specifically called attention to the late Marlowe's blank verse, or as he called it, "Marlowe's mighty line." Indeed, Marlowe's mighty line became the standard of English drama for generations. Marlowe is also the most direct influence on the work of William Shakespeare. Scholars say that if Marlowe had not brought back the tragedy from the brink of extinction, Shakespeare—who rose to prominence immediately after Marlowe—may not have ever even attempted the form in his own works, denying the world *Hamlet*, *Macbeth*, and *King Lear*.

# EDMUND SPENSER

From Castle to Castle

Born in 1552 in London, Edmund Spenser was educated at Cambridge, where he dabbled in writing poetry, mostly sonnets, while training for a career in politics. After serving as a secretary to a lord, he was made a lord deputy during a British conquest of Ireland in 1580. As part of the spoils of war, he claimed and took up residence at Kilcolman Castle, situated in the lands in County Cork that he had helped the English overtake. With little to do all day but sit around and be in charge, he began writing poetry again. He also befriended his "neighbor," the guy in the closest castle: the famed explorer Sir Walter Raleigh. Raleigh brought Spenser along on a visit to the court of Queen Elizabeth, and, wanting a taste of that glamorous lifestyle, Spenser took to writing poetry again with an aim to impress the queen, win himself a place at court, and secure a lifelong pension. Amazingly, it worked: In 1589, he personally presented and recited *The Fairie Queene* for Her Majesty.

This experience ensured that Edmund Spenser would be one of the most highly regarded of all English poets. He wrote in the distinctive, showy style of the late sixteenth century, but his work straddles the very early era of modern English. His poetry, which was as popular as it was masterful, moved the art into a new era.

## FIT FOR A *QUEENE*

*The Fairie Queene* is Spenser's signature work. It's an allegorical, fantastical epic poem through which Spenser glorifies England,

English values, the Church of England, the English language, and everything else with the word "English" in its name. The poem is made up of six books, although the author had intended for it to be twelve, but never finished because he was having too much fun enjoying all the accolades for the first six.

The plot of the poem goes as follows: A prince named Arthur—who represents the Aristotelian ideal of "magnificence" or gentle-manliness, and not coincidentally shares a name with King Arthur—has a vision of the resplendent Fairie Queene—who represents both the concept of glory and Queen Elizabeth. Queen Elizabeth is alternately referred to throughout the poem as Britomart, Belphoebe, Mercilla, and Gloriana. Arthur aims to win her heart, and so recruits twelve of her knights to go off on an adventure on each of the twelve days of the Fairie Queene's annual twelve-day festival. Each of the knights also explicitly represents a different English virtue or value:

- The Redcrosse Knight—holiness
- Sir Guyon—temperance
- Sir Britomart—chastity
- Sir Campbell and Sir Triamond—friendship
- Sir Artegal—justice
- Sir Calidore—courtesy

The poem was written in a poetic structure that Spenser invented for *The Fairie Queene* and which now bears his name. A *Spenserian stanza* consists of eight lines in iambic pentameter (ten syllables), followed by a ninth line called an *alexandrine*, which consists of twelve alternately accented syllables. The rhyme scheme is certainly tough to write in, but to the ear it's rhythmic and satisfying: *ababbcbcc*.

He didn't create this structure out of thin air, though. Spenser based his format on the Old French *ballade* style (poems divided into eight-line stanzas with a rhyme scheme of *ababbcbc*), the same scheme utilized by Chaucer in "The Monk's Tale" in *The Canterbury Tales*. Spenser also owes a debt to classical Italian romance poetry, particularly how the poem is divided into books and then into *cantos*. Nevertheless, *The Fairie Queene* demonstrated that English was an intricate and established language, meaning it was ripe for exploration and pushing the poetic form. In doing so, Spenser created a fresh and distinctly English form of poetry. (And it also earned him a sweet pension: £100 a year for the rest of his life.)

## Quotable Voices

"What though the sea with waves continuall
Doe eate the earth, it is no more at all;
Ne is the earth the lesse, or loseth ought:
For whatsoever from one place doth fall
Is with the tyde unto another brought:
For there is nothing lost, that may be found if sought."

—*The Fairie Queene*

# POLITICALLY INCORRECT

The first three books of *The Fairie Queene* were published as a single volume in 1590, and the next three were published together in 1596. Combining nationalism with masterful poetry made for two bestsellers, prompting publishers to dig up Spenser's minor work composed in college and for periodicals and publish those, too. *The*

*Fairie Queene*'s success afforded Spenser the opportunity to pursue writing full time. While he continued to write long poems to critical and commercial success, he moved into highly political pamphlet writing. In 1596, he wrote *A View of the Present State of Ireland.* An inflammatory tract looking back on his time in Ireland, he argued that the Irish people were impossible to conquer due to their curious languages and customs, and must be exterminated. While that is highly problematic today, to say the least, Spenser's pamphlets provide information about the British occupation of Ireland in the sixteenth century, not to mention the historical context that informs his more acceptably nationalistic English poetry.

# BEN JONSON

Publish or Perish

Ben Jonson was born on the fringes of London in 1572. His father, a minister, passed away just a few months before his birth. Jonson was educated locally, too poor to attend one of the major universities, and upon adulthood he worked as a bricklayer alongside his stepfather. He quit bricklaying to join the army and was stationed in Flanders. Then he returned to London and joined Philip Henslowe and the Admiral's Men, a London theatrical troupe, in 1597. He both acted in and wrote plays for the company and it was here that his career began in earnest.

## Literary Lessons

It's said that Jonson hated working as a bricklayer and that while he worked he consoled himself and entertained his coworkers by reciting *The Iliad* and *The Odyssey*.

Jonson's career in the theater didn't go terribly well at first. His first major play, *The Isle of Dogs* (cowritten with pamphleteer and all-around political agitator Thomas Nashe), was banned after its first performance in 1597 and the script was subsequently lost. It purportedly openly mocked the queen and a prominent baron; for his role in writing the play, Jonson was imprisoned for a few months on charges of sedition and slander.

The following year, in 1598, Jonson killed another actor in a duel, but he begged for mercy from the Church of England and narrowly avoided the hangman's gallows, though he did spend a brief time in prison for the crime (again, just a few months). Upon his release from prison *that* time, he returned to the theater, where he quickly wrote *Every Man in His Humour* for the Lord Chamberlain's Men acting troupe. (The star of the play: some young actor named William Shakespeare.) It was a massive hit and Jonson became the toast of the London stage. The play started a fad for *humours* plays, or comedies in which eccentric characters represent one of the four temperaments or humours:

- Melancholic: represented by the body fluid of black bile
- Phlegmatic: represented by phlegm
- Choleric: represented by yellow bile
- Sanguine: represented by blood

Another big hit in that subgenre was *Every Man in His Humour*'s sequel, *Every Man Out of His Humour*, produced in 1599. With those plays, as well as *Cynthia's Revels* in 1600, Jonson continued to inject satire and dark, even mean, comedy into the Elizabethan theater.

## Quotable Voices

"For this I find, where jealousy is fed,
Horns in the mind are worse than on the head."

—*Every Man in His Humour*

# TRYING ON MANY *MASQUES*

Jonson's feelings about the Crown were complicated, to say the least. Even though he'd satirized the royal family to the point of imprisonment earlier in his career, he went to work at the court of Queen Anne in 1604, writing her a play called *The Masque of Blackness*. Masques, in which ornately costumed actors would perform plays (with musical interludes) in front of elaborate sets, were a popular form of entertainment in the royal courts of Europe at the time. Jonson wrote *The Masque of Blackness* per Anne's request—she'd wanted to star in a play as an African woman. In spite of that (or perhaps because of it), Jonson's next play was *Eastward Hoe*, a play that so mocked the Scottish that Queen Anne's Scottish husband, King James I, threatened to have Jonson's nose sliced off of his face. Jonson emerged from this scandal unscathed by providing information to the king's Privy Council concerning what he knew in regards to Guy Fawkes's failed Gunpowder Plot. Jonson, perhaps feeling indebted, went to work as the court poet for King James, where he primarily wrote more masques. Though not officially given the position, Jonson was, for all intents and purposes, the poet laureate of England.

## Quotable Voices

> "Is shame fled human breasts? That with such ease,
> Men dare put off your honours and their own?
> Is that, which ever was a cause of life,
> Now placed beneath the basest circumstance?
> And modesty an exile made, for money?"
>
> —Celia, *Volpone*

The years of 1605 to 1614 would be Jonson's most prolific period, in which he wrote well-received dramas such as *Epicoene, or the Silent Woman*; *The Alchemist*; and *Bartholomew Fair*. His most famous piece was the comedy *Volpone*. Set in Venice, it allegorically satirized the superficial, wealth-obsessed merchant classes of London.

# GOING TO PRINT

Ultimately Jonson's legacy may be the very concept of leaving behind a legacy. A relentless self-promoter and self-mythologizer, Jonson was the first playwright to have his complete theatrical works (*Works*, 1616) published in the *folio* format—and he's the one who made that publishing endeavor happen. Folio is a publishing technique that saves on paper costs by printing four pages of text onto a single large piece of paper, and then folding the paper in such a way as to create a small book. It's one of the first ways that mass production of books was possible.

Jonson understood what it meant to have one's works in printed form. Not only did it give his writing a sense of permanence, but it gave it an air of importance. The conventional opinion of the seventeenth century was that literature was printed because it was important. Plays were delivered on stage as entertainment and were considered frivolous and ephemeral. Jonson instantly and simply made plays important by publishing them. To drive the point home, he wrote a title page for his collection, comparing himself favorably to the ancient Greek playwrights, who wrote in the other era in which plays were collected in written form. Like Sophocles and Aristophanes, Jonson's plays endured more than other, more popular playwrights of the era. Because of Jonson, Shakespeare's plays were collected as well. If Jonson hadn't published his works, it's arguable that all of the plays from the Elizabethan era could have been lost forever.

# WILLIAM SHAKESPEARE

The Bard

William Shakespeare was born in April 1564 in the village of Stratford-upon-Avon and was educated at a local free school. He married Anne Hathaway in 1582 (at the time pregnant with his child) and moved to London ten years later to earn a better living. Within two years he was acting and writing for Lord Chamberlain's Men, one of the most popular theatrical troupes of the time. By the end of the decade, he was the most celebrated writer in English drama.

## Quotable Voices

"Some are born great, some achieve greatness, and some have greatness thrust upon them."

—*Twelfth Night*

Shakespeare is the first playwright since antiquity to create works that surpassed the classics of Greek drama. In fact, he elevated playwriting with his own work, and nobody has since come close to matching him in terms of scope, variety, or popularity. William Shakespeare is almost universally regarded as one of the best writers in the history of the English language. He excelled at multiple forms of writing, from comedies to tragedies to histories to poetry. Shakespeare is even credited with introducing the concept of character development. He allowed his characters to show their motivations as they shaped the action both organically within the world of the play and in ways that were true to life.

He was also among the first non-classically educated writers to rise to a position of literary greatness in England, due to his natural talent and the work ethic he learned in the hardscrabble world of the Elizabethan theater industry. In fact, he was such an outsider to the literary establishment that rumors still persist that he didn't write all of his own plays, or that an uneducated man simply couldn't have written as well as he did. Shakespeare honed his craft by writing more than two plays a year, presenting them, and editing them for future productions and publication. He was a humble, jobbing playwright who rose to prominence by creating and starring in the most popular theatrical entertainments of the day. His work was seen as little more than entertainment, but he single-handedly elevated the English language and theater to the highest place it had ever been. But he did entertain, and in doing so created literature for the common man, and subsequently, everyone else.

## THE PLAYS

Shakespeare endures not just because of how he wrote, but also because of what he wrote: relatable stories about universal themes. While his characters were more often than not royals, aristocrats, or historical figures, that's ultimately beside the point—he presented characters that dealt with complex problems and issues, such as mortality, power, love, and fear. And he somehow did it all within the strict confines of iambic pentameter, the poetic form in which each line consists of ten syllables, of which every other syllable is stressed. He was a remarkable storyteller but was never bound to one form like most writers are, even the great ones. Shakespeare was as adept at tragedy (*Macbeth, King Lear, Romeo and Juliet*) as the ancient Greeks, but he could also write grand adventure like Jonathan Swift or Daniel Defoe (*The Tempest* and *Pericles, Prince of Tyre*); romantic comedies (*As You Like It*, *The Taming of the Shrew*); and thoughtful, fact-based plays (*Henry V*, *Richard III*) that lent depth and humanity to historical icons. Few writers can boast multiple classics in a single genre; fewer still have written multiple classics in multiple genres.

## Quotable Voices

> "He was not of an age, but for all time!"
>
> —Ben Jonson in the preface to Shakespeare's collected works, the *First Folio*

Shakespeare was also a great editor. He frequently pulled plots from or remade plays by other writers, rendering those plays almost forgotten. For example, Thomas Kyd was a popular predecessor of Shakespeare, and his work *The Spanish Tragedy* was a frequently produced crowd-pleaser. Be that as it may, *The Spanish Tragedy* inspired *Hamlet*, which has been called the greatest achievement in dramatic literature.

# FROM THE GLOBE TO ALL AROUND THE GLOBE

Shakespeare was an aggressive champion of the theater, and he was involved in its business as well as the creative side. When his company lost the lease on its usual performance space, he built the Globe Theatre, an open-air theater with a rectangular stage that held up to 3,000 spectators and charged three different ticket prices (one, two, or three pennies) depending on proximity to the stage.

So universal and resonant were the themes and characters in his works that Shakespeare's plays remain among the most produced in the English-speaking world to this day. These range from traditionally staged productions in New York City's Shakespeare in the Park or by London's Royal Shakespeare Company to wildly creative adaptations. The 1996 film *William Shakespeare's Romeo + Juliet* is set among warring Miami gangs; the classic Broadway musical *West Side Story* is an adaption of *Romeo and Juliet*, too.

## Literary Lessons

The English language literally wasn't big enough for Shakespeare to express the breadth of his ideas. So he invented new words—hundreds of them. Shakespeare used more than 17,000 different words in his plays, of which 10 percent were brand new that he created to fit the situation. They uncannily fit into the language and were instantly understood and adopted into the vernacular. Among the more than 1,700 words Shakespeare is credited with inventing are *advertising*, *bedroom*, *blanket*, *bump*, *compromise*, *critic*, *exposure*, *fashionable*, *gloomy*, *hobnob*, *lonely*, *majestic*, *mimic*, *submerge*, *swagger*, *zany*, and the name *Jessica*.

Also keeping Shakespeare's legacy alive is a new Globe Theatre. In 1989, the original foundation for the long-ago-destroyed theater was uncovered near the Thames River in London. In 1997, a re-creation of the Globe reopened on almost the original spot about 400 years after the original Globe's first production. The play performed on the opening night of June 12, 1997, was one of Shakespeare's most popular histories, *Henry V.* That was also the play that opened the original Globe back in 1599.

# THE SONNETS

As if his contributions to theater weren't enough, Shakespeare made huge strides in English poetry, too. Consider the sonnet.

Generally speaking, a sonnet is a poem of fourteen lines in iambic pentameter. The Petrarchan sonnet, invented by the Italian poet Petrarch in the early 1300s, consists of an *octave*—eight lines with a rhyme scheme of *abba*, repeated—and then a *sestet* of six lines in a different rhyme scheme, often *cdecde* or *cdcdcd*. Contrast that with the Shakespearean sonnet: three separate *quatrains* (a set of four lines) make a point, and a couplet summarizes. The rhyme scheme is *abab, cdcd, efef, gg*.

## Quotable Voices

> "Shall I compare thee to a summer's day?
> Thou art more lovely and more temperate:
> Rough winds do shake the darling buds of May,
> And summer's lease hath all too short a date;"
>
> —"Sonnet 18"

Early-sixteenth-century poet and aristocrat Henry Howard, Earl of Surrey, actually wrote in the sonnet form used by Shakespeare but Howard's work never gained much traction and had fallen out of favor by the time Shakespeare began writing sonnets. Shakespeare's sonnets were so effective that this form is now called a Shakespearean sonnet. Shakespeare wrote and published 154 sonnets, dedicated to "Mr. W.H." (whose identity remains unknown to this day), and almost all of them are an exploration of romantic love.

# Chapter 3

# The Restoration and Beyond

To understand the literature of the seventeenth and eighteenth centuries, you have to understand what was going on in English history during this time period, which was the nation's most chaotic and violent era.

The English Civil War (1642–1651) was fought over the nature of government: an absolute monarchy (in which a king or queen had all of the power) versus a commonwealth (in which the people, by way of elected or appointed officials, have the power). Those in favor of a commonwealth won, and as a result King Charles I lost his head and Oliver Cromwell was placed in charge of the country. The new way didn't work either, and after a decade as Lord Protector, Oliver Cromwell was beheaded, albeit posthumously.

King Charles II, son of King Charles I, the last ruler before Cromwell, was crowned in 1660 and restored the monarchy to England. It's an event now known as the Restoration. King Charles II had spent his exile in France, and upon his return he brought French culture into English culture: massive wigs, fancy clothes, and an appreciation for decadence and leisure. The writers of the era, of course, were skeptical of this new jubilant attitude. They spoke for those scarred by all of the political and actual battles of the recent past. In literature, this skepticism manifested as satire (Henry Fielding), a call to return to classical ideals (Alexander Pope), and a curiosity about the great big world outside of England (Daniel Defoe).

But then Charles II died in 1685 and was succeeded by his Scottish Catholic brother, King James II. Those who feared that England would return to oppressive rule from afar by the Catholic Church instigated the "Glorious Revolution" and installed Protestant noble William of Orange of the Netherlands on the throne. He quickly approved a Bill of Rights, which limited a monarch's power and increased the power of Parliament. That system dovetailed nicely with the Age of Enlightenment sweeping across Europe and England in which thinkers like John Locke advocated a scientific approach and a dedication to reason in all things, including the underlying idea that all men are equal. Those optimistic philosophical themes, as well as a sense that humanity was finally "waking up" to its true nature is pervasive in the literature of the era, in everything from the crusading satire of Jonathan Swift to the thoughtful, divinity-based poetry of John Milton.

# JOHN MILTON

Paradise Found

John Milton is ranked just below Shakespeare as one of the most treasured authors of the English language. Writing primarily about religious themes and man's difficulty in reconciling the secular with the spiritual, Milton's work was not as varied in theme or format as Shakespeare's, but what he lacked in variety he more than made up for in ambition. With his magnum opus *Paradise Lost*, Milton crafted the definitive epic poem of the English language, marrying the classical form with modern techniques and the modern language. *Paradise Lost* expands on the experiments in blank verse undertaken by Christopher Marlowe two generations earlier, confirming the direction that modern English poetry would take: a de-emphasis on rhyme and an emphasis on the expression of emotion and character through descriptive text and lyrical delivery.

Milton's beginnings were humble. He was raised by a father who was a scribe by trade but whose passion was composing music. Encouraged to pursue his passions (which he could because the family was wealthy), Milton attended Cambridge, where he studied divinity and classics. Toward the end of his time at the university, he tried to marry the two, writing poetry about religious themes in Latin, and then secular subjects in English, and then both solely in English. Among his first works was a poem in 1628, "On the Death of a Fair Infant Dying of a Cough," a eulogy for his niece, followed by "On the Morning of Christ's Nativity." Written on Christmas in 1629, it's a baby step in his development, but it bears the hallmarks of what would define his future work: It's meticulously broken down into stanzas, utilizes a lot of proper names, and his physical descriptions of even otherworldly concepts are extremely vivid.

Upon leaving Cambridge with a master's degree in 1632, Milton decided to once again study both divinity and classical poetry because he still couldn't make up his mind. Living at his father's country home, Milton wrote poetry extensively while mastering Latin, Greek, Hebrew, French, Spanish, Italian, and Old English enough to comprehensively study each language's literature. He also traveled, wrote a few short poems, and became a pamphleteer, writing about progressive causes such as freedom of the press the right to divorce, and even justifiable regicide.

## Literary Lessons

Milton was firmly on the side of Oliver Cromwell during the English Civil War. When Cromwell became Lord Protector, Milton was appointed Minister of Foreign Languages. When the monarchy was restored in 1660, Milton was arrested for his involvement with the Cromwell government, but was released on his own recognizance back to his country house, where he settled in to focus on a project he'd been working on intermittently since 1639: *Paradise Lost*.

# AN EPIC JOURNEY

John Milton knew that he wanted his life's work to be an epic poem of some sort and he wrote *Paradise Lost*. After rejecting an idea about the history of England, he decided on something with an even larger scope: the fall of man from the grace of God as it relates to Adam falling victim to the temptation of Satan and Lucifer's expulsion from Heaven. Lucifer is a complicated, contradictory, and even sympathetic character in *Paradise Lost*, which was first printed as a ten-book series (later revised to twelve) in 1667. A towering achievement of epic poetry in English, this poem presents and debates theological themes while also being motivated by the author's feelings, a concept that would inspire the romantic movement a century later. The types of rich characterizations and elaborate language found here were generally not found in epic poetry, which was usually quite dry—it can be quite difficult to express complex emotions within strict meter. Milton got around that by using blank verse.

## Quotable Voices

"The mind is its own place, and in itself
Can make a heav'n of hell, a hell of heav'n."

—*Paradise Lost*

For a 1674 reprint, Milton added a prologue called an "Argument." It includes a summary of all twelve books, along with a defense of blank verse as a poetic form, or "why the poem rhymes not," as Milton puts it. He noted that rhyming lines wouldn't add anything to the work. "Rime being no necessary Adjunct or true Ornament of Poem or Good Verse," he writes, "in longer works especially, but the Invention of a barbarous Age."

Just four years after *Paradise Lost* was published, Milton published a four-book sequel, *Paradise Regained*, depicting the temptation of Christ in the wilderness. It reconciles the original's theme (and what Milton shows as man's spiritual burden) of paradise being lost when Adam and Eve fall prey to Satan, with Man's redemption at Christ's resistance of Satan. Additionally, the character of Satan changes in the sequel. While just as vividly rendered, he's no longer sympathetic, but slimy and slick—the commonly accepted cultural conception of the devil.

Milton didn't make a lot of money off of his masterpiece (or his subsequent sequels) although it had been a publishing hit. Approved and distributed by the Church of England, it was licensed (as all books at the time had to be) for publication by Thomas Tomkins, chaplain to the archbishop of Canterbury, and printed by Samuel Simmons. Milton was so eager to publish that he accepted £5 for the rights, and another £5 after the initial print run of 1,300 copies was exhausted. After Milton's death in 1674, his wife sold away all future rights to *Paradise Lost* for a mere £8.

# JOHN LOCKE

Creating a New Age

Among the most influential books on eighteenth-century world affairs were John Locke's *An Essay Concerning Human Understanding* and *Two Treatises of Government*. His words sparked nothing less than a thought revolution across multiple disciplines, especially philosophy and world politics. They are complex works, but at their hearts, the books are Locke's analysis of *empiricism*: the way the mind gains knowledge by observing, experiencing, and processing experiences. That may sound like a simple concept, but it's merely a jumping-off point to some logical extensions and deep ramifications, including a complete overhaul of the way the English monarchy ruled.

Born in 1632, Locke took on the career of an academic, holding various positions at Oxford. He ultimately became a man of science and served as the house physician for Anthony Ashley Cooper, 1st Earl of Shaftesbury, in 1667. He got his first real taste of the politics that would shape his work when he had to flee to the Netherlands for five years due to his employer's involvement in an attempt to assassinate King Charles II. Locke returned to England in 1688 to serve on a government trade council, and that's when he started thinking seriously about the philosophic underpinnings of politics and leadership.

A crucial shift in the English monarchy also informed Locke's writings: the 1688 Glorious Revolution, in which King James II (a Catholic) was overthrown by a coalition of members of Parliament who installed Dutch royal (and Protestant) William of Orange on the throne, along with his wife, Queen Mary II, who was the daughter of King James II. Most relevant to Locke's work was the new king's support of the Bill of Rights of 1689, which ended forever the absolute power of the British monarchy and instead set up a system in which the monarch would have strict oversight from Parliament.

# GOVERNMENTAL AFFAIRS

In 1690, Locke wrote *Two Treatises of Government*, which outright rejected the once accepted notion of the divine right of kings, or the idea that reasonable kings and queens would rule fairly because they were infallible and had God on their side. Instead, Locke argued, a strong nation in a state of peace required a social contract between the governed and the government, as a ruler is "only a fiduciary power to act for certain ends, there remains still in the people the supreme power to remove or alter the legislative when they find the legislative act contrary to the trust reposed in them." Seventeenth-century English philosopher Thomas Hobbes influenced the social contract Locke outlined in *Two Treatises of Government*. In his 1651 book *Leviathan*, Hobbes argued that a social contract was necessary for a civil society, and that political power must represent the will of the people, and that all men are naturally equal.

## Quotable Voices

"Men being, as has been said, by nature, all free, equal and independent, no one can be put out of this estate, and subjected to the political power of another, without his own consent."

—*Two Treatises of Government*

Locke added in a caveat: that if a government fails to oblige its citizens, its power must be limited. If this is not agreeable, that government can and must be overthrown and replaced with one that recognizes the humanity and natural rights of its citizens. Locke believed the government should protect its citizenry's rights to "life, liberty, and estate." This idea would be echoed in the Declaration of Independence, in which Thomas Jefferson—who had read many of Locke's works—held that men were entitled to "life, liberty, and the pursuit of happiness."

## TOWARD A GREATER *UNDERSTANDING*

The idea behind *An Essay Concerning Human Understanding* (1689) came to Locke when he was debating another topic with a friend and they couldn't come to a place of agreement. He realized that to make progress he first had to examine the idea of human understanding itself. He wrote that it was:

> "necessary to examine our own abilities, and see, what objects our understandings were, or were not fitted to deal with."

This essay stressed that the philosophical examination of how and why the mind works must come before any philosophical examination of the world, humanity, and relationships. In other words, one must figure out how the mind works before one analyzes or even creates art. He believed that the mind puts together experiences, analyzing and comparing and combining them in any number of ways to construct the relationships of ideas that create knowledge, which suggests that knowledge is as subjective as experience.

Locke's theories coalesced into the concept of empiricism, which stood in stark contrast to the absolute rule of monarchs, but fit in nicely with the long-held concept of English self-sufficiency. English readers saw themselves in the ideals of natural equality and the self as a blank slate that gets filled in with accumulated experience. This is just one example of how Locke, a man of science, applied scientific ideas to philosophy.

## Quotable Voices

"The acts of the mind, wherein it exerts its power over its simple ideas, are chiefly these three: 1. Combining several simple ideas into one compound one, and thus all complex ideas are made. 2. The second is bringing two ideas, whether simple or complex, together, and setting them by one another so as to take a view of them at once, without uniting them into one; by which it gets all its ideas of relations. 3. The third is separating them from all other ideas that accompany them in their real existence: this is called abstraction, and thus all its general ideas are made."

—An Essay Concerning Human Understanding

# CHANGING THE WORLD

Locke's ideas didn't just influence other literature and writers—his writings changed the way the world operated. That makes them as influential as the Bible, other religious texts, the Magna Carta, or the Bill of Rights. The message went *beyond* the books. Locke's philosophies were applied to theology, religious tolerance, educational theory, and the rise of the more democratic political systems that would chip away at the British Empire. Locke directly inspired the Enlightenment, a philosophical movement in which *reason* was the overlying motivation and goal, and his writings advanced the concepts of liberty, progressivism, the separation of church and state, and the consent of the governed. Locke's readers realized that things no longer had to be the way they always had been.

# DANIEL DEFOE

Robinson Crusoe

Daniel Foe was born in 1660, the son of a prominent London wax and candle merchant. His childhood was marred by some of the most tragic things to ever happen to London, which would inform the themes of disaster—and survival—in his work. In 1665, the Great Plague of London killed 70,000 people, about a sixth of the population. The following year, the Great Fire of London further decimated the city; only three houses in Foe's neighborhood didn't burn down, his family's being one of them. Foe's life was further turned upside down in 1670 when his mother died.

Because his parents were Presbyterian dissenters—a Church of England splinter group—Foe was barred from attending the two big national universities, Oxford and Cambridge. Instead, he studied at Morton's Academy (a Presbyterian-sympathetic school), the first stop in a picaresque life of adventure not unlike that of Moll Flanders or Robinson Crusoe. After considering becoming a minister, Foe took a job as a traveling hosiery salesman in Spain, France, and the Netherlands. It was around this time that Foe added the prefix "De" to his name to sound more French, and thus more aristocratic. He claimed to be a descendent of the prominent "De Beau Faux" family, which is a clever but not very subtle joke—*faux* is French for "false."

After marrying an heiress, Defoe supported an ill-conceived 1685 revolt against the Crown led by the Duke of Monmouth. He was pardoned, and became close with William III (William of Orange), the new monarch crowned in 1688. Defoe became a spy for the king, but a low point in English-French relations led to losses in his merchant business internationally, which led to huge debts, and then debtors' prison. Following his release, he became a wine trader in Portugal, and returned to England to run an unsuccessful brick factory in the last half of the 1690s. Around £17,000 in debt and fearing a return to prison, Defoe decided to try to write for money. In 1701, he published some poems along with a pamphlet called "The Shortest Way with the Dissenters" that satirized the Church of England's policies toward dissenters, advocating death to the church's enemies. That got Defoe arrested and jailed, but after he was released he worked as a journalist and a pamphleteer under a pseudonym. Over the next twenty years, he turned out more than 400 books and pamphlets.

# A NOVEL IDEA

Defoe is a titan of English literature because he popularized the modern novel—which he didn't even attempt until he was nearly sixty years old. But it was quite the attempt: In 1719, he wrote *Robinson Crusoe*.

## Literary Lessons

The first novel in English was *The Pilgrim's Progress*, written by John Bunyan in 1678, but the concept of long-form, nonmetered prose to tell a single story didn't take off as a format until the huge success of *Robinson Crusoe*.

Inspired by the real-life story of a deserted castaway named Alexander Selkirk, *Crusoe* follows a familiar story pattern: Crusoe's youthful rebellion leads to retribution (shipwreck), repentance (isolation on an island), and then redemption (he returns home). The way

Defoe wrote the story is incredibly innovative. It's told in the first person, not in the distant, removed voice of a third-person narrator. The first-person method was so original that Defoe presented the book as if it was actually written *by* Robinson Crusoe; Defoe claims to be just the editor and, in the preface, calls the book:

"a just History of Fact . . . neither is there any Appearance of Fiction in it."

The full title of the novel reinforces the idea: *The Life and Strange Surprizing Adventures of Robinson Crusoe, of York, Mariner: . . . Written by Himself.*

Defoe's characters are memorably and vividly rendered with lots of visual clues for the reader to embrace. Crusoe carries an umbrella, and his constant companion is a parrot. His sidekick, the island native Friday, is introduced with a huge footprint in the sand, and Crusoe rescues him from cannibals. Crusoe and Friday are likely the first in a long line of great duos in English literature—descendants include Jekyll and Hyde, Holmes and Watson, and Jeeves and Wooster.

The growing middle class of England (which was increasingly literate) made *Robinson Crusoe* a sensation. It wasn't stuffy or cold like previous British literature—it was exciting, salacious, and adventurous. Here the reader is privy to Crusoe's thoughts and feelings, which are a little bit journalistic, and also conversational. It draws the reader into the world of the novel and the mind of the narrator, allowing the reader to experience the visceral events of the novel vicariously.

The book was so successful that Defoe published a sequel, *The Farther Adventures of Robinson Crusoe*, just four months later. By the end of the nineteenth century, the original novel was the most published, translated, and reworked book in the history of the English language. More than 700 different versions of *Robinson Crusoe* had been published.

## Quotable Voices

"I could not forbear getting up to the top of a little mountain and looking out to sea, in hopes of seeing a ship; then fancy a vast distance I spied a sail, please myself with the hopes of it, and then after looking steadily, till I was almost blind, lose it quite, and sit down and weep like a child, and thus increase my misery by my folly."

—*Robinson Crusoe*

With *Robinson Crusoe*, Defoe established so much of what is now commonplace in literature. He invented the standard English novel format, and in doing so proved that fiction was as viable a literary form as the poem. Ultimately, *Robinson Crusoe* is the birth of commercial fiction, or books for regular people, and not just the highly educated.

# JONATHAN SWIFT

The Sultan of Satire

Not much is known about Jonathan Swift's early years, but what is known speaks to the idea of flying by the seat of one's pants to succeed, and of a cruel society aching to be satirized by writers like Swift. Swift's father, a clergyman, died a few months before Swift was born in Ireland, and his English mother left Swift and his siblings behind and returned home. He entered Trinity College in Dublin in 1682 and barely graduated, and then left for London to work as a secretary for a lord and to attend Oxford. Swift then returned to Ireland to earn his Doctor of Divinity at Dublin University. Eventually he was ordained in the Church of England and assigned as the parish priest for a church outside of Belfast.

When he began writing, Swift laid the groundwork of literary satire: broad, approachable comedy that deceptively, and often allegorically, criticizes its target with an eye toward change. It's an insidious tool, but in a good way: Literature and humor help the medicine of a controversial argument go down. By being entertaining, a satire plays to baser instincts and still manages to sneak in a message. Swift made the medicine go down very easily, wrapping his messages in a frothy blend of sex, violence, adventure, and wit to spare.

## MAKING A POINT

Swift's first works of satire didn't concern human rights the way his later works did. In fact, *The Battle of the Books* (1704) is a mock epic about a fight for superiority between classical and modern education. In this short tale, Swift's books come to life and fight each other; he came down on the side of the classics. Swift also published *A Tale of a Tub* in 1704. In this satire, three brothers—who represent the Catholic Church, the Church of England, and the concept of nonconformism—quarrel nonstop.

## Quotable Voices

"I have been assured by a very knowing American of my acquaintance in London, that a young healthy child, well nursed, is, at a year old, a most delicious, nourishing, and wholesome food."

—"A Modest Proposal"

It was Swift's experiences living in Belfast that would inform his humanist satire. He witnessed firsthand what life was like for the subjugated lower classes of Ireland under English rule. One particular piece of Swift's satire still ranks among the most perfect entries in the form. In 1729, Swift anonymously published the essay "A Modest Proposal." Swift's intent was to mock the callous attitude the English held against the poor and starving in occupied Ireland. He did so by taking that hatred to absurd levels, suggesting with a straight face and a measured hand that the Irish could ease their economic troubles by selling their many children as food to the wealthy. The brutal satire here is that rich English people are so cruel to the Irish that they might as well eat their young, because they're subhuman. Great literature can affect change by getting to the hearts and minds, and with his satirical writings, Swift made the foreign, distant, and exotic real and urgent to readers. Swift also positioned satire as a "check and balance." Idealism ran rampant during the Age of Enlightenment, and essays like this one wouldn't allow those in charge to get too self-congratulatory—a legacy of satire that persists to this day.

# TO LILLIPUT AND BEYOND

Swift's most famous work is the sprawling adventure novel *Gulliver's Travels*. Today, it's widely viewed as a children's novel, which speaks to Swift's ability to create literature that works on multiple levels. On the surface, it is a rollicking and fantastical tale, but when Swift was alive, the novel was accepted for what he intended it to be: a wide-ranging satire that mocked everything from English politics to human nature.

The book is split into four distinct travels:

- In Part I, Gulliver shipwrecks on Lilliput, a land inhabited by people that are tiny but incredibly arrogant with a corrupt political system and a lust for power. (This was Swift mocking the English, who, like the Lilliputians, he considered pathetic but also dangerous.)

- In Part II, Gulliver travels to Brobdingnag, or the land of giants. Captured like an animal, Gulliver must explain the human experience to the giant king, who upon review determines Gulliver to be subhuman. He then manages to escape.

- In Part III, Gulliver visits a futuristic utopian city called Lagodo. A send-up of Enlightenment thinkers, scientists have free reign in Lagodo, and they've turned desolate farmland into barren wasteland, having elevated the pursuit of knowledge above ethics and faith.

- In Part IV, Gulliver is caught up between a race of dumb animalistic humans called the Yahoos and intelligent, rational horses called Houyhnhnms.

Swift started writing *Gulliver's Travels* in 1720, shortly after the huge success of Daniel Defoe's similarly adventurous *Robinson Crusoe*, but the book wasn't published until 1726 when it sold out its first printing in under a week. Before agreeing to release *Gulliver's Travels*, publisher Benjamin Motte heavily edited the book to protect himself and Swift against prosecution for a novel Motte considered so satirical that it bordered on slander. The full, true version of the novel wasn't seen until 1735, when Irish publisher George Faulkner published Swift's complete works, of which Volume III was an uncut *Gulliver's Travels*, based on a working copy of the original manuscript. Both versions remain in print nearly 300 years later.

## Literary Lessons

Swift disowned Motte's edited version of *Gulliver's Travels*, which was so altered that Swift said he "hardly know mine own work."

# ALEXANDER POPE

An Un-Enlightened Man

The most important English poet of the early eighteenth century, Alexander Pope (1688–1744) represented a resistance to the free-wheeling progressivism of the Age of Enlightenment. Pope was skeptical of a society so eager to abandon the principles and cultural foundation that it had been building for hundreds of years, and with his work he struck out at what he felt was an increasingly frivolous society and literary landscape.

Part of the disenfranchised Catholic minority, Pope was pushed further to the fringes from almost the beginning of his life when a childhood bout of tuberculosis left him just four and a half feet tall and with a curved spine. Nevertheless, he became a prolific poet equally proficient in satire, aesthetics, and philosophy. Because of his religion, he was barred from England's top schools, and so at age twelve he entered into a program of self-study and took private lessons in the classical languages. And while his family were *personae non grata* in many halls of society due to their faith, they were connected enough to have former secretary of state Sir William Trumbull as a family friend. Trumbull encouraged Pope's talent, and introduced him to William Wycherly, William Walsh, Lord Somers, and other luminaries of the English literati.

## EMULATING THE CLASSICS

Pope published his first work, *Pastorals*, in 1709 at the age of twenty-one. A collection of nostalgic, backward-looking pastoral poetry, it was also an homage to Pope's idol, the ancient Roman poet Virgil, who himself had debuted with a collection of pastoral poems, entitled *Eclogues*. Choosing to present himself to the world first in that way was a statement: Pope's philosophy toward writing was that poets ought to preserve, refine, and conservatively add to the literary legacy left before them. He rejected modern society's environment as it related to art; the rise of commercial literature, especially, didn't mesh with Pope's opinion of the legacy of English poetry.

Pope expressed his artistic philosophies in the poetically formatted *An Essay on Criticism* (1711). In favor of his neoclassical aesthetic, it's also notable for Pope's witty *epigrams*, or short, witty quotations. For example:

- "A little learning is a dangerous thing."
- "Fools rush in where angels fear to tread."

It's a critical essay on the nature of criticism itself—a warning to hold back and analyze before trudging forward. Pope was outspokenly anti-Enlightenment, preferring to find values in the idealized past rather than the uncertain and haphazard future, and the way in which Pope would satirize his shallow literary contemporaries would be with a mock epic poem.

# THE MOCK OF THE *LOCK*

Since he was a young man, Pope had intended to write a straightforward epic in English that would emulate Virgil's *The Aeneid*. Instead, he ended up writing a mock epic to satirize his own age—he didn't feel the Enlightenment deserved to be commemorated with a real epic. That mock epic was *The Rape of the Lock*, issued as two cantos in 1712 and expanded to five cantos two years later. Essentially a devastating eye roll in the form of a poem, this story of a young suitor who cuts a lock of hair from Belinda, the rich woman he is courting, was inspired by actual events that he heard about from a family friend. Pope delivers the poem with all the grandeur of a Homeric tale, treating two quarrelsome families torn apart by a minor and bizarre action of a creepy man with a crush as if they were the Greeks and Trojans fighting over the honor of Helen of Troy. Pope somewhat intended to reconcile the two real-life families by showing them how silly they were behaving, but he ultimately succeeded in creating a brutal send-up of England's upper classes.

## Quotable Voices

"Yet graceful ease, and sweetness void of pride,
Might hide her faults, if Belles had faults to hide:
If to her share some female errors fall,
Look on her face, and you'll forget 'em all."

—*The Rape of the Lock*

In discussing trivial matters in the epic form, Pope draws an unfavorable comparison between his contemporaries and the classical poets. Pope's characters are representative of his England: shallow, vain, morally ambiguous, and deeply confused. (At one point, Belinda thinks an actual rape would be better than the loss of her hair, because it would be a private humiliation instead of a public one: "Oh hadst thou, cruel! Been content to seize / Hairs less in sight, or any hairs but these!") The wealth of these families, says Pope, has led to moral decline and a separation from God and history, something he thinks ought to be considered as the Enlightenment continued on and inspired English imperialism.

Pope heavily favored the definitively English ten-syllable iambic pentameter with rhyming couplets (the heroic couplet) in his work. And he was versatile with it—both *The Rape of the Lock* and *An Essay on Criticism* employ the structure to very different ends. It's also the meter and format Pope used for future poetry, including the rural-celebrating *Windsor Forest* (1713) and his retelling of the famous twelfth-century love story *Eloisa to Abelard* (1717).

An unofficial poet laureate in the 1720s, Pope took his stated role as defender of the English literary tradition very seriously. Among his other major projects, he translated the two extant Homer epics, *The Iliad* and *The Odyssey*, into English and edited collections of Shakespeare plays. Pope, however, was as biased as he always was—he edited the words of the Bard, "improving" them he said, by presenting them in a more neoclassical way.

# HENRY FIELDING

King of Comedy

Henry Fielding was born in 1707 into a family on the fringes of the aristocracy, but with his good fortune came the bad: an early tumultuous life that served as an inspiration for the main character in *The History of Tom Jones, a Foundling*, Fielding's groundbreaking comic novel. Fielding would develop the novel as a respected literary form—and the dominant one at that—consisting of equal parts art and entertainment.

## WHAT A FARCE

At age eleven, Fielding's mother died and his father left the family home in Somerset for London, leaving Fielding and his two sisters behind with their mother's parents. When the elder Fielding married an Italian widow, he called for his children, but the in-laws wouldn't give them up. In 1722, after three years of legal wrangling, a judge ordered the children to stay with their grandparents. Young Henry inherited the family fortune and used some of it to attend Eton College, one of the oldest (founded in 1440 by King Henry VI) and most prestigious boarding schools in England. At the school, he earned a reputation as a womanizer and libertine but not a degree. He left school at age seventeen, but still absorbed classical literature, learned Greek and Latin, and dabbled in playwriting.

Poor financial decisions led to the Fieldings losing most of their fortune in the late 1720s, forcing Henry Fielding to drop out of Leiden University where he was studying in the Netherlands and into the working world of London. For a classically educated man such as himself, this meant writing for the booming entertainment industry: the London stage. His first play, *Love in Several Masques*, was a light comedy and a minor hit. The play was performed at Drury Lane in 1728 and was published that same year. He followed up *Love in Several Masques* with more comic plays, such as *The Temple Beau* and *The Author's Farce*. Fielding found his niche with these silly, over-the-top farces, and he wrote and published twenty-five plays in eight years.

While he reportedly found these plays to be frivolous and disposable, Fielding was undeniably honing his skills of telling amusing stories of flawed characters via comedy. As his characters became more complex in the 1730s, his work grew darker and more satirical. *Pasquin* called out the corruption and bribery in Robert Walpole's government, and *The Historical Register for the Year 1736* was so vitriolic that Parliament passed the Licensing Act of 1737, which required the approval of the Lord Chamberlain before any play could be staged in London. That effectively killed theatrical satire—and Fielding's playwriting career.

## A JOKE MADE SERIOUS

Under the pseudonym "Captain Hercules Vinegar," Fielding took his anti-Walpole sentiment to the page with a newspaper called *The Champion* from 1739 to 1741. It was then that a prominent London printer named Samuel Richardson published a hit novel called *Pamela: or, Virtue Rewarded*. Thousands of Londoners bought it, but Fielding was not a fan. He found *Pamela* to be sentimental, self-serving, and morally simplistic. In response, Fielding anonymously published *An Apology for the Life of Mrs. Shamela Andrews* in 1741. In both books, the main character preaches constantly about her virtues, resists lecherous suitors, and finally marries; Fielding's was presented with exaggeration and jest.

## Quotable Voices

"As he went along, he began to discourse very learnedly, and told me the Flesh and the Spirit were too distinct Matters, which had not the least relation to each other. That all immaterial Substances (those were his very Words) such as Love, Desire, and so forth, were guided by the Spirit: But fine Houses, large Estates, Coaches, and dainty Entertainments were the Product of the Flesh. Therefore, says he, my Dear, you have two Husbands, one the Object of your Love, and to satisfy your Desire; the other the Object of your Necessity, and to furnish you with those other Conveniences. (I am sure I remember every Word, for he repeated it three Times; O he is very good whenever I desire him to repeat a thing to me three times he always doth it!)"

—*An Apology for the Life of Mrs. Shamela Andrews*

Intended as a lark, the direction into satirical prose became Fielding's greatest strength, and with it he developed the skills that would make him a master comic novelist. He parodied a Richardson sequel to *Pamela* about Pamela's brother—which follows the same plot, only with a virtuous male, *The History of the Adventures of Joseph Andrews and His Friend Mr. Abraham Adams*. The main characters Joseph and his travel companion Parson Adams get into many amusing adventures while traveling through Europe in this picaresque novel, which was as much influenced by *Don Quixote* as it was the *Pamela* series. Fielding would take that approach, along with the omniscient and lightly critical narrator device, into several more novels, particularly his masterpiece, *The History of Tom Jones, a Foundling* in 1749.

This novel tells the life story of an impetuous and likeable scoundrel, a literal bastard with a lot of love to give—he's big-hearted, but weak-willed, a sentiment that fuels the comical romance episodes of the book. It's also notable that it's a literary work not about a prominent individual but a regular person, and not even a regular person but an orphan from the lower class who raises his station in life. These concepts were both new and irresistible to the middle-class readers who snatched up the novel, which combined the picaresque with humor, romance, and a mockery of social climbers. It was undoubtedly an influence on major authors of later centuries, particularly George Eliot and Charles Dickens.

## Quotable Voices

"An author ought to consider himself, not as a gentleman who gives a private or eleemosynary treat, but rather as one who keeps a public ordinary, at which all persons are welcome for their money."

—*The History of Tom Jones, a Foundling*

# SAMUEL JOHNSON

Master of the Dictionary

By the middle of the eighteenth century, English had grown into a major world language with an impressive and varied canon of literature. As a literature develops, critics are needed to evaluate those works and to place them in proper context, in history, in society, and in relation to other art. Samuel Johnson (1709–1784) made himself the first major critic, and guardian, of English literature and the English language. His career in letters was varied, and prolific, so much so that he became the subject of one of the first modern biographies, *The Life of Samuel Johnson*, written in 1791 by his friend and traveling companion James Boswell.

## Quotable Voices

"He had no settled plan of life, nor looked forward at all, but merely lived from day to day. Yet he read a great deal in a desultory manner, without any scheme of study; as chance threw books in his way, and inclination directed him through them."

—*The Life of Samuel Johnson*

Piecing together the descriptions of Johnson from Boswell's biography, we know that Johnson was an off-putting and physically unique individual. He was abnormally tall and hefty, blind in one eye, heavily scarred, and flatulent. Johnson was also prone to palsy attacks and verbal outbursts, suggesting he had Tourette syndrome. He was so imposing that it led him to leave his job as a teacher in his hometown in Staffordshire and head to London to be a writer and editor. In the city, Johnson worked extensively, writing critical essays and reviews for various periodicals as well as plays, poetry, and translations of classics. In 1744, he wrote his first major work of nonfiction, *Life of Mr. Richard Savage*, a biography about a friend and popular poet of the era. Johnson enjoyed a reputation among the London literary community as reliable, prolific, and staggeringly knowledgeable.

## WORDS, WORDS, WORDS

By the 1740s, books were no longer rare and precious objects due to the rise of the printing press and mass publishing. (Which is to say nothing of the widely available maps, pamphlets, newspapers, instructional texts, etc.) But despite the massive volume of printed materials in English and a spirited literary community, commonly accepted rules of grammar, spelling, and even definitions of words were not codified or universally agreed upon by writers and editors. An authoritative, definitive dictionary was needed by the English publishing industry as the final say on the mechanics and usage of English.

In 1746, a consortium of London printers and booksellers sought out Johnson to write an exhaustive and accurate compendium of English words, their definitions, and how they were used. No single printer could afford the undertaking themselves, so they approached Johnson as a team.

For his trouble, Johnson was paid £1,575, or about $225,000 in today's money. Johnson (and the printers for that matter) thought the project would take three years, an audacious estimate as it had taken forty writers in the Académie française forty years to assemble the French *Dictionnaire*. Ultimately it took Johnson until 1755—nine years—to compile *A Dictionary of the English Language*. He had a few clerks assist with research and dictation, but otherwise the dictionary is entirely Johnson's work.

## Literary Lessons

*A Dictionary of the English Language* would prove hugely influential, but it was also quite literally huge: It was made up of two volumes totaling more than 2,300 extra-large eighteen-by-twenty-inch pages. It cost £1,600 for the first print run (more than Johnson was paid to write it). A copy of the set ran £4, or about $700 in today's money.

Johnson delivered on breadth and scope. There are 42,773 entries, with each word defined and described in meticulous detail. For example, the entry on "put" runs 5,000 words. Johnson lists twenty different definitions for "time," and 134 for "take." In trying to record the language of the time, Johnson's definitions are in plain, often humorous English, contrary to the blunt, pedantic style generally used in dictionaries. This is his definition of "oats": "a grain which in England is generally given to horses, but in Scotland supports the people." And yet, when economy will do, Johnson obliges. "Sock" is defined as "something put between the foot and the shoe."

And while it was a massive undertaking, the dictionary is still not a complete collection of English words, even for the 1700s, and that's by Johnson's design. While he included many "vulgar" terms (including "fart") and even made up quite a few words, Johnson let his anti-French bias show—virtually all words of French origin were left out of the dictionary, including "champagne."

## Literary Lessons

The full name of Johnson's dictionary, as printed on the title page of the first edition was *A DICTIONARY of the ENGLISH LANGUAGE: IN WHICH the WORDS are deduced from their ORIGINALS, ILLUSTRATED in their DIFFERENT SIGNIFICATIONS by EXAMPLES from the best WRITERS. To Which Are Prefixed, a HISTORY of the LANGUAGE, and an ENGLISH GRAMMAR.*

# LEGACY OF A LANGUAGE

Johnson introduced the now standard dictionary practice of illustrating how the word is used in speech. Every entry received an example of how it's used with at least one literary quotation. Johnson provided more than 114,000 quotations from more than 500 authors; his most frequent sources were Shakespeare, John Milton, the poet John Dryden, and Jonathan Swift. However, if the quotation didn't illustrate the meaning of the word to Johnson's exact needs, he'd just alter the quote.

## Quotable Voices

"To the praises which have been accumulated on *The Rape of the Lock* by readers of ever class, from the critick to the waiting-maid, it is difficult to make any addition. Of that which is universally allowed to be the most attractive of all ludicrous compositions, let it rather be now enquired from the what sources the power of pleasing is derived."

—*Lives of the Most Eminent English Poets*

Johnson's became the standard dictionary for the proper usage of words until Noah Webster's first *Webster's Dictionary* was published in 1828, and was the most exhaustive collection of English words until the *Oxford English Dictionary*, completed in 1928, supplanted it.

How does a writer follow up the definitive account of his entire language? By making an encyclopedia of its best writers. Toward the end of his life, Johnson's last major work was *Lives of the Most Eminent English Poets*, a multivolume collection of biographies of the major British poets. The real heft of the books comes from Johnson's lengthy take on each writer and his works. Always a critic.

# Chapter 4

# The Romantic Era

The romantic era is perhaps the most famous and definitive period for poetry—the image of a "poet" that likely comes to mind is of a romantic, a dandy writing a tortured love poem or lamenting man's cruel and complex nature in between romancing ladies in corsets.

Lasting from the 1790s to the mid-1800s, the romantic era fundamentally shifted English poetry. The novel had supplanted verse as the medium for narratives, so the poem became less about story and more about emotion. This was an experimental and extremely progressive approach to poetry, and an all-out rejection of the reason-obsessed Enlightenment. Romantic poets valued passion over reason and expressed a need to explore the human as an individual, not humanity as a whole. If previous centuries of poetry related what humans did, poetry in the romantic era expressed how one particular poet felt. Truth, it would seem, was subjective and unclear. As romantic poet William Blake said, "To generalize is to be an idiot. To particularize is the alone distinction of merit." This approach persists today. Novels and memoirs are unique and special not just because of their plots but because of who wrote them, and how.

Despite those themes, and a passionate, lyrical quality of pure emotions turned into words, romanticism was not a concerted movement, even though many of the major players worked closely together. (William Wordsworth and Samuel

Taylor Coleridge collaborated frequently; Percy Bysshe Shelley and Mary Shelley were married.) As such, there is often little in common among the work of the individual poets, who range from the pleading to the subtle to the aloof to the very, very dark. That's a variety befitting the celebration of the individual, innate in romantic poetry.

# WILLIAM WORDSWORTH

Emotional Accessibility

The tenets that would define romanticism were developed at the end of the eighteenth century primarily by two poets who worked together and evaluated each other's work: William Wordsworth and Samuel Taylor Coleridge. Wordsworth, the romantic most associated with nature and purity, struck out in favor of emotion-driven poetry in 1798 with the simply but directly titled *Lyrical Ballads*. As he explained in the preface of an 1802 revision of the book, his intent was to present:

> "incidents and situations from common life, and to relate or describe them, throughout, as far as was possible in a selection of language really used by men."

Romanticism needed this commitment to accessibility, because the poems themselves were about poet-specific responses to the world. In his preface, Wordsworth also pre-emptively defends romanticism's favoring of "low and rustic life" because nature offers simplicity and a sense of "elementary feelings."

Those ideas turned poetry conventions upside down. Rather than follow the strict demands of poetic structure, Wordsworth took a stand for natural speech and simple themes, rejecting the English poetic legacy of symbolism, conceits, and allegory. He aimed to use poetry to express emotion over reason, and beauty instead of meaning (because meaning was arbitrary and subjective).

# MAN VERSUS MANKIND

In *Lyrical Ballads*, Wordsworth calls out the work of his contemporaries (and predecessors), specifically the "gaudiness and inane phraseology of many modern writers." Wordsworth's approach was most certainly shaped by the French Revolution. He had lived in France in the early 1790s, post–French Revolution in the early days of the Republic. He was somewhat soured on humanity when England declared war on France in 1793, and tried to reconcile his distaste and disappointment for man as a whole with his deeply held conviction that the individual possessed unique greatness. After early poems such as "The Ruined Cottage" and "The Pedlar," he met Coleridge and they worked together on *Lyrical Ballads*, which begins with Coleridge's "The Rime of the Ancient Mariner" and concludes with Wordsworth's "Lines Written a Few Miles above Tintern Abbey." By and large, the poems explore nature as a conduit to honest expression of emotion.

## Quotable Voices

"Of present pleasure, but with pleasing thoughts
That in this moment there is life and food
For future years. And so I dare to hope,
Though changed, no doubt, from what I was when first
I came among these hills; when like a roe
I bounded o'er the mountains, by the sides
Of the deep rivers, and the lonely streams,
Wherever nature led; more like a man
Flying from something that he dreads, than one
Who sought the thing he loved."

—"Lines Written a Few Miles above Tintern Abbey"

# SAMUEL TAYLOR COLERIDGE

Rhymes and *Rimes*

Samuel Taylor Coleridge was the youngest of ten children born to a clergyman in Devonshire. A gifted student, he began school at the age of three, and at the age of ten was sent to live in a boarding school for orphans after his father died. In 1791, eighteen-year-old Coleridge enrolled at Cambridge University where he stayed until the French Revolution proved too much of a distraction. Then the emotional, idealistic young Coleridge joined the French uprising. He wasn't much of a soldier, but he won favor among the other fighters by ghostwriting love letters to his fellow troops' wives and girlfriends.

## Quotable Voices

"And I had done a hellish thing,
And it would work 'em woe:
For all averred, I had killed the bird
That made the breeze to blow.
Ah wretch! said they, the bird to slay,
That made the breeze to blow!"

—"The Rime of the Ancient Mariner"

In 1797, Coleridge, by then a budding poet and critic, sought out Wordsworth to be friends and collaborators. He was something of an opportunist; Wordsworth's reputation preceded him, and Coleridge thought working together would be a mutually successful idea. It was and together they worked on *Lyrical Ballads*, the first version of which came out in 1798. Primarily a Wordsworth work, it contained Wordsworth's "Lines Written a Few Miles above Tintern Abbey" and "The Prelude," originally titled "Poem to Coleridge."

Coleridge's most famous poem, "The Rime of the Ancient Mariner," didn't appear until the second edition of the book was released in 1800. Highly emotional and visceral in its imagery, it's about the eternal struggle of man against nature. (Although some experts think the poem is full of symbolism over Coleridge's guilt on being part of a nation involved in the slave trade.) Coleridge also introduces the concept of an "albatross around the neck"—a sailor kills the bird and endures bad luck, and it would become a symbolic phrase for the ages.

## TRULY DIVINE

The differences between Wordsworth and Coleridge are slight, but very important to the history of poetry and how romanticism would shake out. Each of the major romantics had a forte: Lord Byron was concerned with passion, for example, and Wordsworth was enraptured by nature, childhood purity, and the power of memory. Coleridge's contribution to the school of romanticism was a fascination with the very idea of imagination. He considered it the highest of all poetic qualities, an almost divine gift, the possession of which made a poet less a conduit of truth than a demigod. His other major area of exploration was the relationship between the inner life and the outside world. Coleridge sought connections between emotions and physical reality, and he believed those moments of transcendence above regular life could be obtained in poetry. In "The Eolian Harp" he uses images of nature to explore the inner workings of the mind.

## Literary Lessons

Coleridge introduced many new words into the English language. Among them are *psychosomatic*, *selfless*, and *bisexual*. Coleridge's definition of *bisexual* was not that of a person attracted to both sexes, but rather one who had the qualities of both genders.

# AN UNRELIABLE MEMORY

In 1797, Coleridge had a very vivid dream while under the influence of opium. When he woke three hours later, he started to write it down as best he could. That work, "Kubla Khan," wasn't published until 1816, upon the urging of Lord Byron. It's believable that Coleridge was inspired by a dream, because the poem feels dreamlike. Imaginative and detailed, the poem describes Xanadu, the royal palace or "pleasure dome" of the titular Mongol emperor, as well as the heavenly landscapes and rivers that surround it.

## Quotable Voices

"But oh! that deep romantic chasm which slanted
Down the green hill athwart a cedarn cover!
A savage place! as holy and enchanted
As e'er beneath a waning moon was haunted
By woman wailing for her demon-lover!"

—"Kubla Khan"

Coleridge is also notable for what could have been. While he was a prolific poet and essayist, he left behind many unfinished projects, frequently missed deadlines, battled a severe opium problem, and was even a chronic oversleeper. He spent several years working on a book of philosophy that he never finished, and he lamented the loss of his original "Kubla Khan"—which he was trying to write after he woke up from his dream, but a knock on his door made him completely lose his train of thought.

## SAVING SHAKESPEARE

Outside of his own poetry, Coleridge's most important legacy is reviving an interest in the works of William Shakespeare. The Bard hadn't disappeared, but over the previous two centuries or so, he'd grown semiobscure. Coleridge's critical work on Shakespeare in *Biographia Literaria*, an 1817 meditation on his favorite writers, reminded English readers especially of how good *Hamlet* was. It was Coleridge who put forth the notion that Shakespeare is the absolute best writer in English, a sentiment accepted as fact by the mainstream ever since. Of Shakespeare, Coleridge wrote: "No mere child of nature; no automaton of genius; no passive vehicle of inspiration possessed by the spirit, not possessing it; first studied patiently, meditated deeply, understood minutely, till knowledge became habitual and intuitive, wedded itself to his habitual feelings, and at length gave birth to that stupendous power by which he stands alone, with no equal or second in his own class."

# JANE AUSTEN

Minding Manners

Jane Austen's classic novels of romance, manners, and realistically rendered female characters were critically acclaimed and were the toast of English high society. Austen was among the first women to have a major impact on English literature, though she wouldn't see that impact. Her books that were published in her lifetime were unattributed. Female authors of the time had to publish anonymously because writing was still looked down on as an unladylike pursuit.

Austen wrote about women's struggles, focusing on themes like a woman's place in a changing society and struggling under those restrictions. She can be associated with the romantics due to her work's emphasis on expressing the gamut of emotions. She upheld the Shakespearean tradition of romantic comedies ending in marriage, but her books were almost exclusively from a female character's point of view.

Austen's father was a rector and she was educated at home. She began to write seriously at an early age (notebooks of her earliest writing, which she wrote between the ages of eleven and seventeen, would posthumously be collected in the mid-twentieth century and published under the title *Juvenilia*). Between the ages nineteen and twenty-two, she wrote drafts of novels that would become *Sense and Sensibility*, *Pride and Prejudice*, and *Northanger Abbey*.

# NOT SO HAPPILY EVER AFTER

Austen wrote in the very early eighteenth century, coinciding with the Regency period of England in which the mentally ill King George III stepped down and his son ruled as the Prince Regent. It's an era defined for its highly stratified class system, including moneyed families regularly connecting over frequent parties and social events. It's this system that Austen chronicles in novels like *Sense and Sensibility* and *Emma*. Austen satirizes snobs and social climbing, but mocks poor breeding in equal measure. She provides strong female characters, while also acknowledging that any advancement they obtained was through marriage. It's telling that she wrote about a class-conscious system in which women had few opportunities besides marrying rich.

## Quotable Voices

"I declare after all there is no enjoyment like reading! How much sooner one tires of any thing than of a book! When I have a house of my own, I shall be miserable if I have not an excellent library."

—*Pride and Prejudice*

Austen's Elizabeth Bennet and Mr. Darcy of *Pride and Prejudice* rank among the great lovers in literature, but it's a miracle they found true love in such a structured society, and despite Elizabeth's protestations and objections. This is very in line with romanticism, as the happy ending of *Pride and Prejudice* doesn't read as "happily ever after." Does Elizabeth truly love Mr. Darcy, or is he simply the most agreeable option for her temperament? The emotions are ambiguous, complicated, and realistically presented.

Only long after Austen's death in 1817 did she receive any sort of literary consideration. The fascination with Austen began in earnest with *A Memoir of Jane Austen*, written and published in 1869 by Austen's nephew, James Edward Austen-Leigh. That legacy, and Austen's status as a giant of English literature, was finally secured in the late twentieth century when adaptations of all of her novels started to hit movie screens, not to mention *Becoming Jane* (2007), a biographical movie starring Anne Hathaway that chronicles the author's formative years.

# LORD BYRON

A Romantic *Don Juan*

George Gordon, Lord Byron, is probably the most definitive poet of all time, both for his extremely emotional verse that defined the romantic era and his flamboyant personality, dashing good looks, and controversial behavior in which the shortsighted activities of the heart often overruled the logical reasoning of the mind—which is kind of what his poetry is all about.

George Gordon was born in 1788, the son of Captain John "Mad Jack" Byron and Catherine Gordon, an heiress to a large estate in Scotland. So as to be able to claim his wife's fortune, Mad Jack changed his and his son's last name to Gordon. The actual hereditary title of "Lord," however, went not to Mad Jack, but to young George, who officially became Lord Byron at the age of ten after his great-uncle, the previous Lord Byron, died. Coming with the title of Lord was a spot in Parliament's House of Lords. The poet would eventually take his seat there at age twenty-one.

By the time he was seventeen, the young Lord Byron had already published a volume of poetry called *Fugitive Pieces* (1806), and he would eventually study at Cambridge and join some prominent literary clubs. While many poets' *juvenilia,* or early, less refined works produced by an author when he or she is just beginning to write, represent an artist still growing and developing his or her style, Byron's was actually quite solidified: Certain poems in the book were so sexually graphic that he was forced to edit them and rerelease the book. (In response, the teenage Byron also wrote a seething critique of stuffy literary critics called *English Bards and Scotch Reviewers.*)

# A HEROIC ACT

Beginning at age twenty-four, Byron made a big impact on the literary scene with *Childe Harold's Pilgrimage*, a narrative poem published in four parts between 1812 and 1818. Byron drew on his own life when writing the poem about a young but already disillusioned and melancholy man tired of a life of luxury and excess who travels far and wide to search for meaning. It was in *Childe Harold's Pilgrimage* where Lord Byron put forth his first so-called "Byronic hero." Now a literary archetype associated with modern-day conflicted protagonists, Harold is a little bit good, a little bit bad, and deeply morally anguished. Harold, as all Byronic heroes are, is an intelligent, handsome, charming bad boy who's somewhat self-destructive due to an unchangeable arrogance, cynicism, and tendency to upset authority figures. If this sounds like Byron, that's no accident—*Childe Harold's Pilgrimage* is largely autobiographical.

# BACK TO BASICS

Lord Byron believed in the unique point of view of the poet as well as the glory of nature, which places him firmly with the romantics. He gained both relevant life experience and enjoyed immense natural beauty as he traveled extensively around Europe in the 1810s, particularly Greece and Turkey. His poetry was as varied as his travel. While he wrote with a romantic philosophy, he rarely stuck to a handful of particular poetic devices. His extensive knowledge of the form allowed him to use whatever technique was appropriate for the topic, a forebear of language-bending modernists like James Joyce. Byron wrote short poems and epics. He used blank verse, heroic couplets, rhyme royal, quatrains—whatever felt right to his heart as he wrote.

> "There is a pleasure in the pathless woods,
>   There is a rapture on the lonely shore,
>   There is society where none intrudes,
>   By the deep Sea, and music in its roar:
> I love not Man the less, but Nature more,"
>
> —*Childe Harold's Pilgrimage*

Use of form aside, Byron looked to the classics more than his contemporaries. His icons were Restoration- and Augustan-era poets, especially John Dryden and Alexander Pope. He liked those poets' use of meter and wit. Byron often wrote of the great conflicts, both internal and external, innate in existence. Among Byron's exploratory subjects:

- nature versus civilization
- oppression and repression versus freedom
- whether all restraints are necessary or superficial

But most of all, Lord Byron wrote about love (and sex). He was a romantic *and* a romantic.

# DON JUAN

In 1819, Byron once again upset the skittish literati with his ribald epic poem *Don Juan*, one of the most significant English epic poems since John Milton's *Paradise Lost*. There were legends of Don Juan before Byron committed him to literary history, but Byron made the lover, the heartbreaker, famous. *Don Juan* is a romantic poem about romance—or the lack thereof. It's a freewheeling, forward-thinking poem mocking the ideal of love and contrasting it unfavorably with the joys of sex. Love, Byron said, was not a natural feeling but an artificial construct of mankind. *Don Juan* was immensely popular, in spite of or because of what one critic called its "immoral content." The work was also widely pirated. When one of the unauthorized publishers was caught, he argued that the poems were so scandalous that they didn't deserve to be copyrighted.

## ISN'T IT ROMANTIC?

Lord Byron was a romantic poet, but first he was a real romantic, which is to say a lady's man and a rogue. He was apparently very handsome and debonair and romanced many women. In 1815, he married Annabella Milbanke, an heiress, but the marriage fell apart due to his constant womanizing.

He was equally careless with his money … and his need to travel wasn't completely artistically motivated. To flee debts, as well as rumors he was having an affair with a half-sister, he left England in 1816 and lived abroad for the remaining eight years of his life. He died in 1824 at age thirty-six, while in the not very romantic midst of planning an assault on Turkey-controlled Lepanto in the fight for Greek independence. He fell ill with a virulent cold, which wasn't helped by the bloodletting the local doctors performed on him to try to improve his condition. Bloodletting is a crude medical procedure dating at least as far back as ancient Greece. Under the theory that the body's fluids are out of balance, blood that is perceived to be excessive is drained from the patient. As you can probably imagine, it doesn't work. But while the bloodletting certainly didn't help him improve, Lord Byron's death was likely due to sepsis—his body shut down after being treated with infection-laded medical instruments.

## Quotable Voices

"And on that cheek, and o'er that brow,
So soft, so calm, yet eloquent,
The smiles that win, the tints that glow,
But tell of days in goodness spent,
A mind at peace with all below,
A heart whose love is innocent!"

—"She Walks in Beauty"

# WILLIAM BLAKE

Burning Bright

The seeds of the romantic movement were planted in Germany in the late 1700s with *Faust*, Johann Wolfgang von Goethe's play based on the Faust legends (as well as English playwright Christopher Marlowe's *The Tragical History of the Life and Death of Doctor Faustus*) about the dangers of man acquiring too much knowledge and floating through life without an emotional connection to his surroundings. Romantic poets explored those ideas and expanded on them, which played out in poetry as paeans to rural life, the need to explore other cultures, and a glorification of the common man.

William Blake was among the first English poets to embrace these concepts in the 1780s and 1790s, even if his contributions to poetry weren't widely recognized until the late 1800s, long after the actual romantic movement had come and gone (and long after his death in 1827). But what he did was monumental: He demonstrated that poetry could be used to explore vague emotional concepts instead of just delivering a narrative, as had been done for centuries.

## TAKING A STAND

Born in 1757, Blake followed a career as a tradesman. He was studying to be an engraver at the Royal Academy but found the rigid environment and teaching style too stifling to his art. Despite not graduating, he set up a business as an engraver and illustrator. He earned a living on commissions and work for printers, but his skills enabled him to publish (in small runs, to little notice) and illuminate his own work. His volumes include *Poetical Sketches* (1783), *Songs of Innocence* (1789), and *Songs of Experience* (1794). Juxtaposing words with images on the same plates allowed Blake to build in extra levels of meaning and intent to his work that other poets couldn't provide—helpful, as he was creating a new genre.

## Quotable Voices

> "I will not cease from Mental Fight,
> Nor shall my Sword sleep in my hand:
> Till we have built Jerusalem,
> In England's green & pleasant Land."
>
> —"Jerusalem"

In influencing the individuality and humanism of romanticism, Blake represents a break from the England-glorifying authors that came before him, such as Alexander Pope and Edmund Spenser. His interests lay not in simply what it meant to be English, but what it meant to be alive. Blake wrote about personal liberty, believed in equal rights for women, rejected the absolute authority of the Church of England, and even advocated free love. For example, his epic poem *Milton* (1810) does glorify England, but not the Crown or imperial might, but rather England's art, as well as the meaning of art itself. Blake is a character in the poem, and he joins forces with a resurrected John Milton to explore in verse the relationship between writers and their influences. The poem's introduction, popularly known as "Jerusalem," sets the tone, praising English art in lieu of the Crown or imperial might.

# BREAKING FREE

Blake thoroughly rejected the aggressive British colonialism of the day, as well as the industrialization that followed. He had little rights in society because he was a poor artist, and he looked hopefully toward the more positive, human-oriented revolutions happening in France and in England's colonies in the New World at the time. Quite often, his character-driven poems are based around a protagonist trying to break free of oppression, be it from government, marriage, or the church. Blake was highly conflicted about many things, particularly religion. For while his poems contain many biblical allusions, he didn't find organized religion particularly palatable, and considered it a separate entity from anything actually spiritual. The alternative, science and rationality, didn't please him much either, for it represented to Blake a repression of the imagination.

Blake's most famous poem, and one that pulls together his questioning of spiritual themes, nature, abstract thought, and personal point of view, is "The Tyger," which originally appeared in *Songs of Experience*. The poem is structurally quite simple: six quatrains arranged in rhyming couplets. Each suggestive section asks another question so as to clarify the first one, which is essentially seeking an answer to "What is the nature of the God that would create an animal like the tiger?" The poem compares a divine creator to a blacksmith, an image that's driven into the mind of the reader through the effective use of the poem's rhythm: The couplets imitate the beat of machinery.

Blake's work has enjoyed a robust second life as the inspiration for some major twentieth-century pop culture. His 1809 painting *The Great Red Dragon and the Woman Clothed in Sun* figures prominently in *Red Dragon*, Thomas Harris's 1981 prequel to *The Silence of the Lambs*. In this book a serial killer is obsessed with the painting, thinks he can transform into the dragon from the piece, and has a tattoo of it covering his back. Lines from Blake's poems even pop up in songs by musicians such as the Doors, Bob Dylan, and U2.

## Quotable Voices

"Tyger Tyger burning bright,
In the forests of the night:
What immortal hand or eye,
Dare frame thy fearful symmetry?"

—"The Tyger"

# HORACE WALPOLE, MARY SHELLEY, AND GOTHIC ROMANTICISM

Scary Monsters and Super Creeps

Nature contains within it great volumes of beauty and wonder as well as terrifying darkness and mystery. And as the romantic poets explored the glory and goodness of nature, gothic romantic writers investigated those natural feelings of moodiness, foreboding, and sheer terror. Romanticism looks at the natural, while gothic romanticism examines the possibility of the supernatural—a turn to the dark side, for sure. Gothic fiction and poetry was intended to instill pleasure by thrilling its audience through an exploration of the dark parts of existence—it's basically Halloween in written form. When gothic fiction veered into the evil, the occult, and the supernatural, it was both fascinating and irresistible to the Victorian society that was supposed to be repulsed by it.

## DOWNRIGHT SPOOKY

At its heart, romanticism represented a turn to the past for some kind of truth. Gothic romanticism also turns to the past, but not to the neutrality and prehistory of nature, but specifically to the medieval. Gothicism embraces and imitates the dark, uneasy feelings often associated with that time period. For that reason, gothic works are almost always set in ancient, dark, and gloomy castles, with their dungeons, secret passageways, unexplained sounds, and adjacent graveyards that might as well be haunted. Those details were symbols of the human feelings of alienation and hopelessness, but they came to be signifiers of the genre itself because they were so thoroughly macabre and didn't provide answers, only mystery. Gothic literature would also play out in the works of Victorian-era authors and define the mainstream novels of the time, particularly Dickens, whose scenes were of urban nightmares, not castles, and the Brontë sisters, whose novels of despair were set in the foggy moors of northern England.

# HORACE WALPOLE

The first true gothic novel, written by Horace Walpole, even has a gothic-sounding title: *The Castle of Otranto*. Published in 1764, it takes place in a haunted castle. There's a tormented hero named Manfred (a Byronic hero decades before Lord Byron came along), who has a secret, some people die mysteriously, a portrait moans in the night, and the characters are overwhelmed with overwrought feelings of anguish, terror, secret keeping, and, because it's still romanticism, passionate love that cannot come to fruition. In other words, all the definitive hallmarks of gothic romanticism are there.

Walpole was inspired to write the novel by the architectural style known as gothic revival, which harkens back to the medieval building style of ornate buildings with high arches and flying buttresses. (Think castles, cathedrals, and old university buildings—that's gothic, or gothic revival, architecture.) The son of prime minister Sir Robert Walpole, Horace Walpole had moved into Strawberry Hill, an estate on the Thames River, and remodeled it with turrets, battlements, arched doors, and other ornamental touches to create a fake medieval architecture. This remodel started a fad in architecture, just like Walpole started the fad in literature, too. Due to Walpole's influence, gothic romanticism would end up becoming the most popular literary genre in England for around fifty years, inspiring the likes of Clara Reeve, Ann Radcliffe, and most notably, Mary Shelley.

# HOW TO MAKE A MONSTER

Born Mary Wollstonecraft Godwin in 1797, Mary Shelley had the philosophy of what it meant to be human and the anguish therein in her blood: Her father was political scientist William Godwin, and her mother was feminist writer Mary Wollstonecraft (who died a month after the younger Mary Wollstonecraft's birth). Raised by her father alone, Mary was privately and extensively educated in literature and progressive political theory. She ran off with romantic poet Percy Bysshe Shelley when she was seventeen, traveled Europe, and had a daughter born prematurely who died in infancy. The couple married in 1816 after Shelley's wife Harriet committed suicide over her husband's affair. Quite the gothic life indeed.

## Literary Lessons

The most definitive and enduring gothic novel of all is Mary Shelley's *Frankenstein; or, The Modern Prometheus*. The title demonstrates how the gothic came from romanticism—it invokes ancient Greek mythology, as Prometheus is a deity in the Greek canon said to have created mankind.

Mary Shelley enjoyed a modest career as a travel writer until her husband enlisted her to be his first reader and personal editor. Together, the Shelleys were part of a legendary circle of romantic poets, and in 1818, the Shelleys and Lord Byron spent a summer together in a house on Lake Geneva in Switzerland. One rainy day, the group passed the time by reading German ghost stories. Mary Shelley was fascinated by the dark, macabre elements, which had long been part of the German literary heritage; the Brothers Grimm wrote their twisted fairy tales in German, for example. Byron suggested a ghost story contest, which inspired the idea for *Frankenstein*.

*Frankenstein* is a thin novel but a dense one that has way more depth than its simple premise would indicate. The story follows a scientist who aims to create a humanoid out of dead body parts, but makes a monster by mistake. But Shelley's book is really about what makes us human, if humans can and should play God, the dangers and limitations of science and industry, and all the other themes the romantics were wrestling with at the time. What makes it gothic are the details: Dr. Frankenstein sneaks around graveyards to rob corpses of their organs and limbs, and he sews them together in a workshop in his dark castle.

## Literary Lessons

Also present at Lake Geneva on the day of Lord Byron's writing challenge was John William Polidori, who wrote "The Vampyre" in 1819. Pulling from eastern European folk tales, he created many of the elements of the modern idea of the bloodsucking vampire. It created a craze for vampire fiction and is the most lasting element of the gothic tradition.

*Frankenstein* can also be considered the first science-fiction novel, despite the lack of science or even mock science in the novel—Frankenstein's monster simply is reanimated, but it isn't explained how. What is present: discussions of the moral issues of humanity and the consequences of creating life.

# ROBERT BURNS

The Scottish Bard

Robert Burns was born in 1759 in the village of Alloway to tenant farmers who made sure their son knew how to read and was well provided with books, particularly the poetry of authors like Alexander Pope. Burns was a true romantic—often falling in love and writing poems about his passion. His first major poem was called "Handsome Nell," written for a young lady named Nellie Kilpatrick. Falling in love hard and often, and then writing verse about it, was a theme that would recur throughout Burns's life.

Burns factors into the English canon as not just one of the major poets of the late romantic era but as a major voice of Scotland. Romanticism coalesced quite nicely with Burns's hundreds of sincere, hard-felt, individualistic odes to the simplicity of Scottish life, including its traditional culture and natural beauty. He also wrote about class distinctions and uniquely Scottish customs and religious practices, and he did it in a Scottish dialect.

## THE TOAST OF SCOTLAND

As much as Burns wrote, he still had to work on his parents' farm. However, he spent as little time as possible on the family business, preferring instead to write poems about nature and romancing local women. He inherited the farm in 1784, but his lack of interest in tending to it made it financially insolvent. By the time he'd impregnated two different women two years later (in addition to the twins he had with his wife, Jean Armour), Burns, the future national poet of Scotland, was about ready to permanently flee for Jamaica. He planned to run away with Mary Campbell, the inspiration for his poem "Highland Mary." But then Mary suddenly died...and Burns's book *Poems Chiefly in the Scottish Dialect* became an unexpected bestseller.

## Quotable Voices

"How sweetly bloom'd the gay, green birk,
How rich the hawthorn's blossom;
As underneath their fragrant shade,
I clasp'd her to my bosom!
The golden Hours, on angel wings,
Flew o'er me and my Dearie;
For dear to me as light and life
Was my sweet Highland Mary."

—"Highland Mary"

He became almost instantly famous for Scottish celebrations such as "Address to a Haggis" and "The Highland Lassie." As tastes for romantic and pastoral poetry grew, Burns's *Poems* with their Scottish backdrop, one of the most romantic and pastoral places in the British Empire, came out at exactly the right time. Burns moved to Edinburgh where he became a star in that city's literary scene, and he was extremely productive there. He wrote more than 300 poems and songs between 1786 and 1789, many collected in the *Scots Musical Museum*, a publication founded to preserve and promote Scottish folk songs and music. Among his work from this time are the New Year's Eve staple "Auld Lang Syne" and "Ae Fond Kiss."

# A NATIONAL TREASURE

Burns made a fortune from *Poems Chiefly in the Scottish Dialect* and other works . . . and he blew it all in eighteen months gallivanting around Edinburgh. In 1789, he returned to his wife (who'd been raising all of his children, legitimate and otherwise) and took a job as a tax collector. His poetry at this time veered into a more political and nationalistic direction, and he wrote his most famous and atmospheric story poem, "Tam o'Shanter" (1791). It's about a man named Tam who angers a coven of witches in Alloway and has to flee on Meg, his old gray mare. A witch named Nannie catches him by the River Doon, but the water overpowers her magic and Tam escapes over a bridge. (Meg isn't so lucky.)

Burns is regarded as the national poet of Scotland, an honor for which he openly campaigned. In 1787, he described himself thusly:

"A Scottish Bard, proud of the name, and whose highest ambition is to sing in his country's service, where shall he so properly look for patronage as to the illustrious names of his native land: those who bear the honours and inherit the virtues of their ancestors?"

In "The Answer, to the Guidwife of Wauchope-House," he adds,

"No nation, no station / My envy e'er could raise: / A Scot still, but blot still, / I knew no higher praise."

Burns was the national poet of Scotland for good reason. Not only was his poetic skill unmatched, before or since his lifetime, but he was so devoted specifically to preserving the literature, culture, and language of Scotland. By the late eighteenth century, the Scottish vernacular was dying, as unity with England led to the widespread adoption of English, threatening the local tongue. It continued to do so in the decades after Burns's death. The poetry of Burns preserved the Scottish dialect for the ages.

Burns died in 1796 at the relatively young age of thirty-seven. He endured a fatal flare-up of rheumatic fever after falling asleep on the side of the road, at night, in the rain, after a night of heavy drinking. He was buried with full Scottish military honors, and a memorial edition of his poems was published to raise money for his many children.

## Literary Lessons

Every January 25 throughout the English-speaking world, poetry aficionados and Scots alike celebrate Burns Night. Started by Burns's friends a few years after his death as a way to honor the "The Ploughman Poet" on the anniversary of his birth, a Burns Night dinner includes feasting on haggis (while "Address to a Haggis" is recited) followed by whisky, readings of Burns's poems, and finally a group rendition of "Auld Lang Syne."

## Chapter 5

# The Victorian Era and the Industrial Revolution

Queen Victoria (1837–1901) had more of an influence on British society and its arts than any other monarch, and she was most definitely the last whose personal morals and choices were widely mirrored by her subjects. The Victorian era was the last time England had a monoculture, before globalism and imperialism would make the idea of "Englishness" far more complex. But writers were already exploring with wringing hands what it meant to be English in the face of an ever-changing and increasingly cruel world. That said, the incredibly structured and divided life of English society, its countless social norms, and the constant anxiety about what other people would think were informed, satirized, and questioned by the literature of the time.

As the ability to read became widely possible and the printing press made books widespread and affordable, the often academic and didactic works of the great poets lost out in popularity to the real, relatable, and reality-reflecting structure and stories of prose. The novel is the legacy of previous populist authors like Henry Fielding and Jane Austen, whose stories got inside characters' heads and put their thoughts right into the heads of readers. And, as is the case with any art, hallmarks and clichés of the form emerged. The dominant kinds of Victorian novels were adventure stories, social satire, and idealized stories in which the good guys won with luck, hard work, and love, and the bad guys were duly punished.

The Victorians romanticized childhood and invented the idea of childhood being a special, specific, and innocent time of life devoted to exploration, learning, and whimsy. And thanks to sweeping school reforms, for the first time in history children were by and large literate, and publishers were happy to provide books for them. Lewis Carroll, Robert Louis Stevenson, and Charles Dickens helped establish the basic form of the children's novel, creating first-person characters who see the world as a child does and capturing that childlike wonder. As for the adults, they wanted big, exciting stories, too. They got them with tales of mystery and the supernatural, exemplified by Sherlock Holmes, Dr. Jekyll (and Mr. Hyde), and Dracula.

**Top:** Illustration of "the Venerable Bede," author of *Ecclesiastical History of the English People*, as seen in the *Nuremberg Chronicle*.

**Bottom left:** Illustration of the Knight from the illuminated Ellesmere manuscript of *The Canterbury Tales*.

**Bottom right:** Vintage engraving of Geoffrey Chaucer, author of *The Canterbury Tales*.

**Top:** Illustration showing King Arthur and the Knights of the Round Table.

**Bottom:** Illustration depicting the death of King Arthur *(Le Morte d'Arthur).*

Photo credits: Getty Images/wynnter and Getty Images/duncan1890

**Top:** R.A. Artlett's engraving of the William Shakespeare "Chandos" portrait.

**Bottom:** The Globe Theatre, a reconstruction of William Shakespeare's famous theater, which was demolished in 1644.

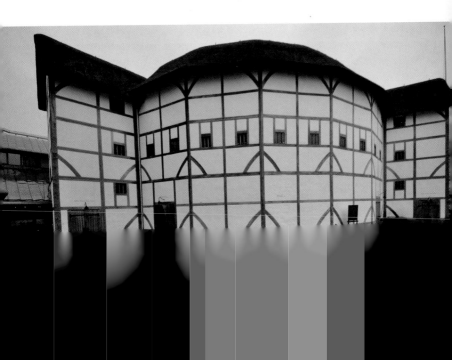

**Top left:** John Milton, author of *Paradise Lost*. **Top right:** Illustration depicting a scene from Jonathan Swift's *Gulliver's Travels*. **Bottom:** Jane Austen's House Museum in Chawton, England. Austen lived here from 1809 until 1817 while she wrote *Mansfield Park*, *Emma*, and *Persuasion*.

**Top:** William Blake's illuminated poem "The Tyger" in *Songs of Experience*.

**Bottom:** Engraving of Charles Dickens in his study at Gad's Hill Place.

**Bottom inset:** John Leech's "The Second of the Three Spirits." A depiction of the Ghost of Christmas Past from Charles Dickens's *A Christmas Carol*.

Photo credits: William Blake (Public Domain) via Wikimedia Commons; Getty Images/kreicher; and Getty Images/Andrew Howe

**Top:** Portrait of Charlotte Brontë painted by Evert A. Duyckinck, based on a drawing by George Richmond.

**Bottom:** Penistone Crags in England, made famous as the meeting place of Heathcliffe and Cathy in Emily Brontë's *Wuthering Heights*.

"*I* GROWL WHEN I'M PLEASED, AND WAG MY
TAIL WHEN I'M ANGRY"

Illustrator John Tenniel's depiction of a scene from Lewis Carroll's *Alice's Adventures in Wonderland*.

**Top left:** James Joyce by Alex Ehrenzweig.
**Top right:** "The Death of Sherlock Holmes"
by Sidney Paget. This image served as
the frontispiece, an illustration opposite
a book's title page, of Sir Arthur Conan
Doyle's *The Memoirs of Sherlock Holmes* in
which Holmes meets his untimely demise.

Joseph Conrad monument in Ukraine, his place of birth. The monument bears an
inscription taken from his novel *Lord Jim*, which reads, "There is nothing more enticing,
disenchanting, and enslaving than the life at sea."

# ALFRED, LORD TENNYSON

It's Good to Be the King

Alfred Tennyson was born in the idyllic village of Somersby in August 1809. Like a kid in the twentieth century who saw *Star Wars* and went out to his backyard with a branch and pretended he was Luke Skywalker with a lightsaber, Tennyson got hooked on the canon of King Arthur legends, which his poetry-loving mother frequently read aloud, and he spent his childhood playing near a stream, pretending he was King Arthur or Sir Lancelot. Those stories, and that literary tradition, would propel Tennyson to an illustrious literary career.

Tennyson's father was mentally ill, epileptic, and an alcoholic, who in spite of all that was a Cambridge-educated minister who ran the Somersby rectory. He insisted that Tennyson only read the classics and pursue a more suitable career, such as the ministry, but Tennyson's mother encouraged him to write his own epic tales. Under her tutelage, he memorized large swaths of *Le Morte d'Arthur* and John Milton's *Paradise Lost*. By the time he was fourteen, he had written his own Arthurian heroic tales of knights, as well as a 6,000-line epic poem and a play in blank verse called *The Devil and the Lady*. At eighteen, he went to Cambridge and, with his brother Charles, published *Poems by Two Brothers*. It wasn't a literary sensation, but it did get him the attention of an underground literary club at the university, which was led by a fellow student named Arthur Hallam. Hallam and Tennyson became close, but Hallam died of a brain hemorrhage in 1833, just six years later. Many of Tennyson's poems were in tribute to Hallam, and Tennyson's son, who would become one of the most important Tennyson scholars, was named Hallam Tennyson. Tennyson credited Arthur Hallam with giving him not only the confidence to write, and to write what he wanted—about King Arthur, and almost only about King Arthur—but also to perform his poems aloud.

## Quotable Voices

> "But in her web she still delights
> To weave the mirror's magic sights,
> For often thro' the silent nights
> A funeral, with plumes and lights
> And music, came from Camelot:"
>
> —"The Lady of Shalott"

Alfred, Lord Tennyson's most striking contribution to the history of England is inspiring a nationalistic fervor and a pride in the country's art. He did it by stoking a revival in the King Arthur and the Knights of the Round Table legends. And that was precisely Tennyson's intent. To him, the King Arthur stories were a major part of the English heritage that contemporary readers ought to embrace because their themes were so relevant to his time period. He called these legends "the greatest of all poetical subjects" because they were about such universal themes as honor and chivalry, and provided realistic character archetypes.

# GOOD KNIGHT

Tennyson's first solo collection of poems, *Poems* (1833), contains a few that focus on King Arthur, and he followed those with long poems such as "The Lady of Shalott," "Sir Launcelot and Queen Guinevere," "Sir Galahad," and "Morte d'Arthur." While these poems celebrate

Arthurian stories and legends, most are Tennyson's own versions of the stories with his own analysis thrown in. For example, in "Sir Galahad," Tennyson's knight is pure and earnest, but characterized by self-analysis and arrogance, and is restless for adventure—a very Victorian idea of a medieval ideal.

Wealthy enough to write full time, Tennyson continued to toil away in the 1830s on little-noticed poems and a poetry collection. Then, in the 1840s he lost his entire inheritance due to some bad investments (which in turn ended his engagement to a woman named Emily Sellwood). But fortunately in 1842, his legacy was secured with the two-volume release of *Poems*. The title is the same as his 1833 release, but it was a completely new collection, and heavy on the King Arthur poems. It was a hit with critics and readers. What did that mean for a poet in England in the mid-nineteenth century? It means he was named the twelfth poet laureate of England, succeeding William Wordsworth. This achievement also helped him win back the love of Sellwood.

Tennyson was now the official poet of the queen, and is in many ways the official writer of the Victorian era. He was the most famous artist and nonpolitical figure in England of his time. He was also a public figure, and struck an imposing look in a long beard, cloak, and wide hat, and read in a booming voice. As poet laureate, he was required to write poems to celebrate England's many industrial and political triumphs. Ironically, the world of politics and the military were not areas in which Tennyson was familiar or even comfortable—he was more in tune with pastoral England. But that's quite the Victorian concept: Tennyson was torn between his duty to a rapidly changing society and his love of the purity and truth of nature and the past. At any rate, the position earned him £10,000 a year, enough to buy a house in his beloved countryside and spend most of his time working on *Idylls of the King*.

# *IDYLL* HANDS

Tennyson started writing what would become his great work, *Idylls of the King*, in 1831 when he was only twenty-two years old. He would ultimately spend decades writing, rewriting, and revising *Idylls*. For example, he finished a twelve-book draft in 1833 as a prose work, but had converted it into a five-act musical pantomime performance piece by 1840. It would eventually be published as a cycle of twelve blank-verse story poems between 1859 and 1885. Tennyson aimed for *Idylls* to be a contemporary "reboot" of the King Arthur legends—the English national epic that Britons could relate to and find depth in—reflecting concerns and problems of his era. *Idylls* is really a declaration of Victorian England notions of idealism and morality, as presented through the lens of the Arthurian legends. The work was a blow against the cynicism and selfishness of the changing era, and it allowed Tennyson's readers to embrace the ideals of the past. All that time Tennyson spent writing was worth it. *Idylls of the King* sold 10,000 copies in its first month. For his contributions to English culture and national pride, Queen Victoria named Alfred Tennyson a lord in 1884. Thereafter known as Alfred, Lord Tennyson, he died just eight years later.

## Literary Lessons

Among Tennyson's non-Arthurian work is "The Princess," a long poem published on Christmas 1847. In the early stanzas of the poem, Tennyson takes the bold stance that women are equal to men and require education and special schools. But as "The Princess" rolls along, Tennyson pulls back a little, arguing that though women are on the same level intellectually as men, they have different natural roles. (By the end of the poem, the hero becomes more masculine, the heroine more feminine, and that is how they both find happiness.)

# CHARLES DICKENS

Charles Dickens (1812–1870) was *the* towering figure of English literature in the Victorian era and the industrial age. His novels and stories provided contemporary accounts of life in nineteenth-century England so vividly that his work has become a living, breathing document of the era, detailed as it was in both descriptive prose and emotional realism. His stories about the lower classes, orphans, and women who had been subjugated by the system (in the form of bureaucratic red tape, the courts, or orphanages, for example) led to actual social and legal changes and an improved social safety net in England.

Dickens's realistic, relatable novels like *Great Expectations*, *Oliver Twist*, and *Bleak House* also coincided with—and helped create—the mass media. In reality, Dickens's novels were the first modern novels, even though many of his works were published in serialized form, at one chapter a month. This was because there was such an instant and dramatic demand for anything the prodigious writer produced. It could be argued that Dickens was a precursor to the celebrity, name-brand authors of the twentieth century.

## LITERATURE FROM EVERYDAY LIFE

Writing about the bleak world of the English lower classes came naturally to Dickens, who experienced subjugation and poverty firsthand during his childhood. After losing two brothers as a child, his family moved to London where, at the age of twelve, he got a job labeling jars in a shoe polish factory. It provided enough money for him to rent a room at a boarding house when his parents were sent to debtors' prison. As Dickens grew into adulthood he worked a variety of jobs, as a law clerk, newspaper reporter, and short-story writer for the then emerging magazine format.

Because Dickens was a man of the people, he wrote for the common man. As recently as the romantic era, reading and writing had been the sole provenance of the wealthy, because they didn't have to work all day, every day. Furthermore, the wealthy and the noble were more often than not the subject of written works. (Even Shakespeare's plays deal mainly with royalty and prominent families.) Dickens's tales of regular people made regular people interested in literature in general, and in Dickens's books in particular.

# BECOMING A CULTURAL AND LITERARY INFLUENCE

Among the nuts-and-bolts innovations of Dickens is the parallel story structure. For example, *The Life and Adventures of Nicholas Nickleby* takes place over many years and involves many characters, some of whom get their own side stories for at least a few pages. This kind of structure allowed for novels that were packed with characters, story, and settings, instead of just one major storyline like the fiction that came before Dickens. Dickens also popularized the use of the flashback (e.g., the Ghost of Christmas Past in *A Christmas Carol*) as a storytelling device. By giving the reader a glimpse into a character's past, Dickens astutely revealed his character's motivation, resulting in well-rounded, more realistic figures.

But most of all, Dickens was the first major novelist to use long passages to describe the physical details of places or people. Prior to this, details were sparse, a tradition passed down by playwrights. The different character names that he chose also reinforced characteristics and in a not-so-subtle way told readers a lot about the character on first read: Mr. Stryver in *A Tale of Two Cities*, for example, is an idealistic lawyer, or a *striver*.

## Quotable Voices

"It was the best of times, it was the worst of times, it was the age of wisdom, it was the age of foolishness, it was the epoch of belief, it was the epoch of incredulity, it was the season of light, it was the season of darkness, it was the spring of hope, it was the winter of despair."

—*A Tale of Two Cities*

His work became part of the identity of the English-speaking world. For example, in Dickens's time, December 25 was a regular day of business in London. That changed with *A Christmas Carol*. Dickens used the grumpy, miserly Ebenezer Scrooge in this novella to show that to not celebrate the holiday with warmth and generosity was wrong. With the novella's "true meaning of Christmas" theme, Dickens argued that Christmas should be nostalgic and sentimental. And again, he pulled this idea from his childhood—he made generations crave a "white Christmas" by ending *A Christmas Carol* with one. It almost never snows in London in late December nowadays, but when Dickens was a boy in the 1810s, it snowed every Christmas.

# Literary Lessons

Have you ever been called a Scrooge? You can thank Dickens for that. The word "Scrooge," obviously referencing his main character from *A Christmas Carol*, Ebenezer Scrooge, was so evocative that it entered modern-day vernacular to mean a grumpy person, particularly one who doesn't enjoy Christmas.

There are only a handful of writers who left such an indelible mark that their name became an adjective. But while "Shakespearean," "Kafkaesque," and "Shavian" describe works influenced by William Shakespeare, Franz Kafka, and George Bernard Shaw, respectively, "Dickensian" breaks through into the real world. "Dickensian" describes a particularly pathetic state of poverty.

# GEORGE ELIOT

Out in the Country

You may have heard the name George Eliot and not realized that the name was just a pseudonym. In reality, George Eliot was well known to be a woman named Mary Ann Evans, but she used the male pseudonym because it was her "brand."

Eliot didn't have the advantages typically thought of as advantages to women in mid-nineteenth-century England—she didn't come from a rich or prominent family and even rejected the "proper" way for a lady to marry. She took up with the married George Henry Lewes, who was unable to get his wife to grant him a divorce. And of course, she was a writer, which was equally, if not more, frowned upon by polite society. That's why she had to establish herself under a male pen name. Eliot was not formally educated, but self-trained herself in adulthood through an increasingly rigorous curriculum of skill building. She translated German philosophy texts into English to learn to pay attention to detail, and then edited and wrote reviews in order to force herself to analyze mechanics and form while also staying abreast of contemporary authors and stylistic trends. When she felt ready, she started writing fiction, beginning with short stories and then moving on to novels.

In 1873, when Eliot was already a literary star, she met with literary critic F.W.H. Myers at Cambridge University. Their conversation turned to what they agreed were the three concepts that most literature was forever exploring: God, immortality, and duty. Eliot's thoughts on the matter, according to Myers:

"How inconceivable was the first, how unbelievable the second, and yet how peremptory and absolute the third."

Her take is representative not only of her own work but of a growing general sentiment in the late Victorian era. As consciousness and technology increased, the world got smaller, and people in England started to doubt their one true faith, or at least the Church of England's interpretation of their faith. While some poets would say that love of other kinds or a return to nature were the replacements to fill that void, Eliot's novels argue that morality can lend meaning to life, even independent of religious dogma.

## GETTING REAL

Especially at the beginning of her career, Eliot wrote what she knew, which is an easier way to wade into writing than by inventing scenarios and people. Eliot became a major Victorian novelist and figure in literary history because her works were profoundly realistic, leading to realism as a full-fledged movement. Eliot's realism (and realism as a movement) is twofold:

- Her work contains subtle, profound psychological insights into human nature.
- Her work also depicted life outside of London, which was overwhelmingly the setting for most English novels. She showed that the towns and the country—where a huge portion of the English population lived—contained just as much drama (and splendor) as the city did.

Like Dickens, Eliot wrote simple tales on the triumph of morality; Eliot just did it about and for country people.

## *MILL* AND *MARNER*

Eliot's first major work is the semiautobiographical novel *The Mill on the Floss* (1860). It depicts a decade in the lives of Tom and Maggie Tulliver, two close siblings growing up in a village in eastern England. In demonstrating the common problems of country dwellers, it explores the conflict between choice and chance. Tom and Maggie's father can't stay financially solvent due to stubbornness, while others' livelihoods depend entirely on the whims of nature. Meanwhile, Maggie grows up and finds a vaguely unsatisfying notion of love.

## Quotable Voices

"In old days there were angels who came and took men by the hand and led them away from the city of destruction. We see no white-winged angels now. But yet men are led away from threatening destruction: a hand is put into theirs, which leads them forth gently towards a calm and bright land, so that they look no more backward; and the hand may be a little child's."

—*Silas Marner*

Next, Eliot published *Silas Marner* (1861), a sparse novella about a lonely miser who loses his gold and nearly his soul but finds redemption through the love of an orphan who arrives at Christmas. Like Eliot's other novels, it celebrates simple lives and ordinary people, and explores the constant interplay between humanity's good side and dark side.

# GLORIFYING THE NORMAL

In *Middlemarch* (1877), Eliot's careful study of provincial life comes alive. One of the most painstakingly realistic novels of the era, it's ironic that Eliot invented the actual town (but not the lifestyle). The action revolves around a cast of seven characters, primarily Dorothea, freshly wed to the much older and very sour Rev. Casaubon. The sprawling novel contains lots of mundane details that don't necessarily serve the plot, but do illustrate the setting, which makes the themes and characters come alive.

## Quotable Voices

"But the effect of her being on those around her was incalculably diffusive: for the growing good of the world is partly dependent on unhistorical acts; and that things are not so ill with you and me as they might have been, is half owing to the number who lived faithfully a hidden life, and rest in unvisited tombs."

—*Middlemarch*

*Middlemarch* veers from past great literary texts in that it's a celebration of the realities of daily life, not big events. It's also notable for Eliot's unromantic depiction of marriage. Where most fiction and plays end at a wedding and a "happily ever after," in *Middlemarch*, Eliot makes marriage a starting point, and shows it as an often complicated journey.

# AN EXPANDING VIEWPOINT

Eliot didn't *always* write about small, semitranquil villages in eastern England. In *Romola* (1863), she branches way out with a novel that was neither contemporary nor set in England. It's a historical novel about the Italian Renaissance set in Florence in the 1490s and follows the massive changes underway in both art and religion.

And *Daniel Deronda* (1876) is a caustic look at national and cultural identity, the nature of Englishness, and the prejudices therein. The title character is an English aristocrat who learns that he's Jewish. He suddenly becomes aware of anti-Jewish sentiment in his country, and at the novel's conclusion he abandons Britain for the Middle East. The novel was controversial, first for the blatant criticism of England, and because it was among the first English novels to feature a Jewish protagonist (thus proving Eliot's accusations correct).

The most innovative aspect of Eliot's prose is that she just can't help but break into the action to chastise characters, comment on the action, or lay out what the reader ought to be feeling. In *Middlemarch*, for example, Eliot nearly screams from the page at the reader to look up and take notice of the misery that surrounds them (except that it might just break them):

> "That element of tragedy which lies in the very fact of frequency, has not yet wrought itself into the coarse emotion of mankind; and perhaps our frames could hardly bear much of it. If we had a keen vision and feeling of all ordinary human life, it would be like hearing the grass grow and the squirrel's heart beat, and we should die of that roar which lies on the other side of silence."

Over her twenty years of publishing novels, Eliot expanded the scope of English literature to include more voices. Not only did she challenge the increasingly silly notion that writing was not a suitable pursuit for women, she showed that people in rural communities had something to say, too. Without Eliot, it would've been significantly more difficult for later literary luminaries like the Brontë sisters and Thomas Hardy to break through.

# THE BRONTË SISTERS

Moor Power

Charlotte, Emily, and Anne Brontë were among a new generation of writers who decided to work at being writers, and to make it their profession, as opposed to the generations of nobles or the independently wealthy who could give writing a shot if the artistic muse so moved them. That provided a working-class (or working poor) point of view, not to mention that they were women. Neither voice had been widely heard in English literature at that point.

The daughters of Patrick Brontë, an Irish clergyman who ran the parish of Haworth on the Yorkshire moors in the northern part of the country, didn't live anywhere near London. The Brontës' popularity, despite their location, foretold the coming century's rise of writers who didn't come from London, live in London, or write about London. Along with George Eliot, they wrote about other places in England, and other people in England, expanding the breadth of the national literature. And as much as their work showcases the world outside of the confines of the city, the Brontës nonetheless had a very real distaste for the world.

## LIFE IN A NORTHERN TOWN

Their Yorkshire moor novels are gothic, dark, and emotionally honest. The Brontës wrote novels based on emotion, when such abstract feelings at the time were largely done in poetry. But they did it with all the definitive hallmarks of gothic fiction, including:

- big houses
- darkness
- spookiness
- a sense of melancholy and doom
- deep, anguished feelings surrounding even good things like love

The settings are visceral, lively, and unforgettable, and the characters psychologically realistic and honestly portrayed. That makes the Brontës among the first feminist authors.

## PSEUDONYM SUCCESS

Their historic careers were almost derailed before they ever began. In 1846, Charlotte Brontë sent a few of her poems to Robert Southey, at the time England's poet laureate. The good news: He read them and wrote back. The bad news: He told her she didn't have a future in literature because she was a woman. Southey wrote:

> "Literature cannot be the business of a woman's life, and it ought not to be. The more she is engaged in her proper duties, the less leisure she will have for it, even as an accomplishment and a recreation."

Undaunted, Charlotte Brontë compiled her best poems, along with those of Emily and Anne, and sent them to the London publishing house Aylott and Jones, who published them under the title *Poems*, by Currer, Ellis, and Acton Bell. Acknowledging the innate prejudice exemplified by Southey, those names are all male pseudonyms; Currer, Ellis, and Acton Bell are the similarly initialed

Charlotte, Emily, and Anne Brontë, respectively. Number of copies sold in the first print run: two.

The Brontës' response to the failure of their poetry? Write novels instead. They would continue to use their pseudonyms, partially as a go-around to the sexist publishing world, and partially because they didn't want any publicity should their books sell well.

## Quotable Voices

> "Do you think, because I am poor, obscure, plain and little, I am soulless and heartless? You think wrong!—I have as much soul as you,—and full as much heart! And if God had gifted me with some beauty and much wealth, I should have made it as hard for you to leave me, as it is now for me to leave you!"
>
> —*Jane Eyre*

# A NOT VERY PLAIN *JANE*

Charlotte Brontë (Currer Bell) wrote half a dozen novels, primarily about a young woman's coming of age and the emotions she experiences along the way, often weighing reason and common sense with passion and following her heart. Prior to later works in this vein such as *Shirley* (1849) and *Villette* (1853) was her first novel: *Jane Eyre* (1847). Emotionally intense and urgent from the title character's point of view—generally seen as hallmarks of poetry—the novel follows the title character's journey from child to adult as she falls in love with Mr. Rochester of Thornfield Hall and develops her own moral belief system. Told from Jane's point of view, and internally at that, it's a major development in narrative form and feminism.

# TO NEW *HEIGHTS*

The Brontë family produced two classic novels in 1847. First *Jane Eyre*, and then Ellis Bell/Emily Brontë's *Wuthering Heights*. *Wuthering Heights* is quite the Victorian novel in that the characters' lives are difficult, but obstacles are overcome through hard work en route to a happy ending. But *Wuthering* is also a callback to the gothic romantic tradition—there are many scenes of characters in anguish, wallowing in self-pity, and lamenting their sinful natures, all while tooling around in a giant, spooky house. Because it's set in the distant moors of northern England, the characters are isolated by geography and disconnected from London society—which doesn't matter much to them. It's one of the few Victorian novels not wrapped up in the London scene. It's acknowledged, certainly—Catherine and Heathcliff are very concerned about how the unseen society lords and ladies will judge their actions—but it's far away, while the characters are present, and now, dealing with their personal issues.

## Quotable Voices

"If he loved with all the powers of his puny being, he couldn't love as much in eighty years as I could in a day."

—*Wuthering Heights*

*Wuthering Heights* is also more of a romantic novel than a Victorian novel in that Brontë delves deep into the minds and hearts of the characters' emotion-driven feelings and motivations. Heathcliff is a violent, emotional wreck, weighing the world on his shoulders. He is a horrifying monster, but also relatable, attractive even, because he rejects the Victorian notion of propriety and feels all of his feelings with gusto.

"The ties that bind us to life are tougher than you imagine, or than anyone can who has not felt how roughly they may be pulled without breaking."

—*Agnes Grey*

## *GREY* DAYS IN THE *HALL*

Anne Brontë (or Acton Bell) also wrote a novel in 1847: *Agnes Grey*. Loosely based on the author's experiences as a governess in Yorkshire, Agnes serves at one wealthy house after another, each full of horrible, disrespectful children. One of her charges grows up to enter into a terrible marriage, Agnes's father dies, and she eventually marries a parson.

In 1848, Anne Brontë wrote her second (and ultimately last) novel, *The Tenant of Wildfell Hall*. One of the first truly feminist novels before such a thing had a name, it concerns Mrs. Helen Graham (née Huntingdon), the wife of an abusive alcoholic who flees with her son to the ancestral home under a false name, pretending to be a widow and selling paintings to earn a living.

## TRAGIC ENDINGS

Each Brontë wrote classic, near-perfect novels for the ages. But as was befitting the true dark, gothic manner in which they wrote, they were cut down in their prime in a bizarre series of tragic events. Tuberculosis spread amongst the Yorkshire house where almost the entire Brontë clan resided. The Brontës' brother Branwell died from the disease in September 1848 at age thirty-one. Two months later, it claimed thirty-year-old Emily Brontë. Over Christmas, Anne contracted what they thought was the flu—it was tuberculosis, of course, and she died at age twenty-nine the following May. Charlotte Brontë outlived them all, but just barely. In March 1855 she died at age thirty-eight after suffering severe dehydration and malnutrition due to typhus.

# ROBERT BROWNING AND ELIZABETH BARRETT BROWNING

The First Couple of Poetry

Victorian poet Robert Browning wrote fluidly and with rich, enduring imagery about art, morality, and change—all major concepts for a country that went from predominantly rural and agrarian to industrial and urban in less than two generations' time. Browning helped the people make sense of it all. He's arguably even more famous for being part of the "First Couple of Poetry," as his wife (and often subject) was Elizabeth Barrett, a champion of the downtrodden and poetic crusader for social change during one of the cruelest periods in English history.

Browning was born in South London in 1812 and had a comfortable home life, the son of a clerk at the Bank of England. More importantly, Browning's father had a private library of more than 6,000 books, which young Browning devoured, and he started writing original poetry at the age of twelve. Around the same time, he grew frustrated with the limitations of his formal private school and sought out a home tutor and educated himself via the library. By fourteen, Browning was fluent in Greek, French, Latin, and Italian, and was intimately familiar with the poetry of the romantics, particularly Lord Byron.

Browning most often presented his poetry as dramatic monologues, like what you would find in a play. Browning utilized imagery and symbols to reveal truths about the speaker and his problem and point of view, and while Browning was heavily inspired by the romantics, he veers off in that the speaker in his poems is a character, not Browning himself (as a playwright would write a dramatic character). In romantic poetry, the point of view of the individual poet was tantamount, and the poems were the truth of that poet.

## SETTING THE SCENE

Browning also invites an audience into the "scene" of the poem in the same way as an audience would be in a play. Characters are a conduit by which Browning explored his thoughts and ideas. That detachment also allowed him personal distance as an author and narrator. It's a technique that would be widely utilized in the twentieth century; for example, T.S. Eliot is not the same person as J. Alfred Prufrock, nor do they necessarily share views.

A recurring theme in Browning's works is the effect of urbanization on the English people. Industrialization meant that the work moved from farms to factories and mills in cities like London and Birmingham, which led to mass emigration to those cities. The results of this emigration?

- Close quarters
- Poverty
- Violence
- Lack of hygiene

Perhaps most importantly for the arts, this emigration to the city resulted in a loosening of strict social mores—at least as far as the working classes and former peasants were concerned. City living was anonymous, which meant there weren't any small-town gossips or relatives to watch and judge. As a result, excessive drinking and sexuality became a common part of daily life. Browning weighed in on these issues, along with the conflict between the freedoms that the city allowed and loss of the social safety net afforded by family and familiarity. Moreover, Browning believed urban life was over-stimulating and numbing. In his works, violence became synonymous with urban life.

Consequently, Victorianism was a conservative response to the chaos and moral impunity of urban life. For Browning this was a jumping-off point for exploring the relationship between art and morality. Did art *need* to have a moral message? He was of the mind that empiricism could be a rational basis for behavior, intellectual and artistic, challenging the religious norm with science.

## A MAN AND A WOMAN OF LETTERS

Browning was not a widely heralded literary figure until much later in his life, in the late 1860s when he was nearly sixty years old. And as influential and important as he was to establishing the foundations of Victorian poetry, his works weren't nearly as popular as those of Elizabeth Barrett. In 1844, her collection *Poems* was released, which included a favorable reference to Browning in the poem "Lady Geraldine's Courtship." Flattered, Browning wrote Barrett a letter, and over the next year and a half the relationship grew from mutual appreciation to romantic as they exchanged nearly 600 letters. In 1845, Browning and Barrett married (opposed by her father, who was against *all* marriage) and moved to Florence, Italy.

Barrett was a social crusader through her work, crafting politically progressive poems that both addressed and offered solutions for a variety of social ills, including the slave trade, child labor, and the general restrictions on everything women did in the 1800s.

Like a Kennedy or a Roosevelt, Barrett came from a wealthy family but was a champion of the underrepresented. Her father owned sugar plantations in Jamaica, and owned a 500-acre estate in Herefordshire called Hope End. In 1810, four-year-old Barrett started to write poetry, and her father nicknamed her "the Poet Laureate of Hope End." By the age of ten, Barrett had read histories of England, ancient Greece, and ancient Rome; most of Shakespeare and *Paradise Lost;* the Bible in Hebrew; and translations of the Homeric epics. Apart from just an occasional tutor who primarily helped her brother, Edward, she was self-taught. She most liked to read more modern philosophers (Voltaire, Rousseau, Wollstonecraft), which created a foundation for her human rights poems, an artistic response to the brutality of the Victorian era. Barrett's first major work was *An Essay on Mind, with Other Poems*, published anonymously in 1826. An ambitious work for a twenty-year-old, its centerpiece was an eighty-eight-page poem that attempted to connect the histories of poetry, science, and philosophy into one unified thread.

## UNFORTUNATE INSPIRATION

In 1832, financial mismanagement of the family's Jamaican plantations led to a loss of Barrett's family fortune and estate. Earlier, at age fifteen, she'd injured her spine when trying and failing to saddle a horse, and seven years later a blood vessel in her chest broke. For the rest of her life, she was chronically weak and had a nasty cough. Once the plantations were lost, her family moved to the seaside town of Sidmouth for Barrett's health, but three years later, she moved to London.

## Quotable Voices

> "But through the storm no moonbeam fell
> Upon the child of Isobel—
> Perhaps you saw it by the ray
> Alone of her still smile."

—"Isobel's Child"

Having never lived in a city before, she was both appalled and inspired. The buildings all looked the same, the streets were filthy, and soot covered everything, an environment that inspired her poems about the need for change and beauty. But it was also the center of English art and literature, and in 1838 she gained entry into those circles with the printing of *The Seraphim, and Other Poems*, which was not published anonymously this time. Critics raved about the long poetic drama about two angels in Heaven retelling Bible stories and commenting on the crucifixion as it takes place. Other poems in the book included the sad and haunting "Isobel's Child," about the death of an infant.

# A CHANGE IS GONNA COME

But just as she was hitting it big, Barrett's health took a turn for the worse and she spent years bedridden, first in coastal Devonshire and then in London. Depressed but wealthy thanks to book sales and an inheritance, she spent her days writing poetry, submitting dozens of poems to English and American journals. Her 1844 poetry collection *Poems* earned the attention of many (not just Robert Browning), particularly due to Barrett's best-known poem, "Lady Geraldine's Courtship." It's about a young, poor poet who falls in love with an earl's daughter. The poet assumes the lady is out of his league, but they get a happy ending after all, in spite of a disapproving, classist society.

## Quotable Voices

> "The young lambs are bleating in the meadows.
> The young birds are chirping in the nest.
> The young fawns are playing with the shadows.
> The young flowers are blowing toward the west:
> But the young, young children, O my brothers,
> They are weeping bitterly!"

—"The Cry of the Children"

A year later, Barrett's "The Cry of the Children" appeared in the periodical *Blackwood's Edinburgh Magazine*. After both reading about and seeing firsthand the deplorable working conditions in mines and factories for child workers, Barrett angrily called out the practices and demanded they change. Thanks to popular writers like Barrett and Charles Dickens advocating for reforms, change would come slowly over the next few decades. Barrett's influence and popularity was such that she was reportedly considered for poet laureate in 1850—an otherwise unthinkable major position for a woman at the time. It wouldn't happen (it just wouldn't be proper for a lady, after all), and Barrett's injuries and sickness would finally claim her life in 1861. Browning outlived her by nearly three decades.

# LEWIS CARROLL

Adventures in Absurdity

The first invention of Lewis Carroll, one of the most inventive authors of all time, was the very idea of "Lewis Carroll." There is no Lewis Carroll—it's a pseudonym created to clearly delineate a separate literary career and character from that of the otherwise serious and sedate clergyman and math professor Charles Dodgson. That's right—the man who created the psychedelic wonderland of *Alice's Adventures in Wonderland* was primarily a mathematician!

As an author, Carroll combined fantasy, wordplay, satire, classically dry British wit, and utter nonsense in his work that commented on and defined the times. His work contained images of delight but confusion and acceptance of the absurdity of life. While they were enjoyed by children and adults at different levels at the time, Carroll's work has come to be associated with children's literature, for his work involves talking animals and the fantastical. But he deserves a place in the British canon for taking literature—and observances of life—to strange, often dark and unsettling places.

## A MAN OF MANY TALENTS

Dodgson was born in 1832 in Daresbury, in Cheshire (the namesake of the Cheshire Cat), one of eleven children born to a Church of England archdeacon. Dodgson had aspirations of following in his father's footsteps, but he also wanted to be a mathematician, and to be a writer. He devoured Shakespeare, Coleridge, and Tennyson as a teenager and wrote and illustrated his own magazine at home called

*Mischmasch.* Ultimately, he was able to follow all three pursuits. Dodgson graduated from Oxford with honors in both mathematics and classics. Beginning in 1856, he was a math lecturer at Oxford.

# DOWN THE RABBIT HOLE

Around 1856, Dodgson became close friends with Henry Liddell, a new dean at the university, and his family. During frequent rowing excursions on the Thames River, Dodgson concerned himself with entertaining the children, joking with them, drawing pictures, and making up fantastical stories, and they all became subjects of Dodgson's photography. Dodgson enjoyed the audience of children: He found they shared his similar absurd and silly sense of humor and didn't mind his stammer; he didn't have many adult friends because they were put off by that same silliness and stuttering problem.

## Literary Lessons

Among the words Carroll made up that entered into common English usage: *chortle*, *galumph*, and *portmanteau*, a word that means two words are combined—like how *newscast* is a mash-up of "news" and "broadcast."

Dodgson so enjoyed composing silly poems and crazy stories off the cuff that he decided to start writing in earnest. While writing half a dozen math books in his lifetime under his own name, his creativity burned and so he started submitting to magazines. To create a separate identity from his Oxford math professor identity, he used the pen name Lewis Carroll. Demonstrating the cerebral wordplay that would define his work, Dodgson got his pen name by translating his first and middle names into Latin, and then back into English in a slightly different form and reversing them. To wit: Charles Lutwidge became Carolus Ludovicus, which became Carroll Lewis, or Lewis Carroll.

During an afternoon picnic in the early 1860s with the Liddell children, Dodgson made up a story about a girl named Alice (named for his favorite Liddell, eight-year-old Alice), who chases a rabbit into a hole in the ground and sets off on a bizarre, surreal adventure involving a mad hatter, a riddle-loving cat, and the Queen of Hearts. Alice Liddell loved the story, and she begged Dodgson to write it down so she could read it whenever she liked. He did, and did her one better: He got it published in 1865 as *Alice's Adventures in Wonderland*.

It didn't get good reviews or sell well at all at first. It was written to entertain children, and written largely spontaneously, so it didn't follow any set literary tradition. In short, it was so completely original and inventive, not to mention weird, that few really knew what to make of it. Critics and readers were dismissive, claiming it to be total nonsense at worst and absurd to a fault at best. One thing that did get praise were John Tenniel's illustrations, which helpfully detailed the madness for the reader. Those images remain a part of the book to this day.

*Alice* caused such an uproar, simply for daring to be different in an age where being different was simply not okay, that readers were tantalized—the book became a bestseller because so many people wanted to see what the fuss was about, or they wanted to experience something fresh and original. Over the next six years, the book's stature increased to the point where Dodgson pitched and published a sequel, *Through the Looking-Glass, and What Alice Found There*, in

1871. By that time, Dodgson was no longer on speaking terms with the Liddells, perhaps because of the nude photographs he had taken of Alice. The sequel was written for a different Alice, his cousin, five-year-old Alice Theodora Raikes.

## Literary Lessons

Carroll wrote children's books and poetry, as well as political treatises like *The Principles of Parliamentary Representation*. He also wrote *A Tangled Tale*. Combining his love of math with silly children's stories, the reader must solve math puzzles to advance in the story. It's perhaps the first example of interactive fiction.

# SPLIT PERSONALITY

While writing his *Alice* books and his academic titles, as well as teaching at Oxford, Dodgson still found the time to publish poetry in periodicals, collected in the 1869 collection *Phantasmagoria and Other Poems*. Later he would write his two most famous and bewildering bits of hallucinatorily absurd poetry: "The Hunting of the Snark" (1876) and "Jabberwocky" (1871).

The *Alice* books and Dodgson's poetry abandon, deconstruct, and reimagine the very ideas of normal logic and natural systems. This is an interesting approach for a math professor, and has led to a lot of theories about the author's motivations and intentions. Some critics think that the *Alice* books are where Dodgson the logical mathematician and Carroll the surrealist converge—they could be seen as one long metaphor satirizing new thoughts in mathematics in the nineteenth century, a world in which Dodgson didn't think held much room for creativity or even interpretation. More often than not, however, there's been much more speculation as to how Dodgson could create such fantastical worlds out of thin air, on his own, out of the blue without the assistance of mental illness or drugs.

Dodgson and Carroll remain an enigma—his papers were burned after his death. A handful of his journals survive, and even those have had pages removed. This has all led to mystery surrounding him, a rare feat for a relatively modern-day author and an incredibly popular and famous one at that.

## Literary Lessons

The psychedelic, surreal, dreamlike-bordering-on-nightmarish, things-are-not-what-they-seem world of Lewis Carroll has had a huge influence on twentieth-and twenty-first-century art and popular culture, from music (from "White Rabbit" by Jefferson Airplane to "Wonderland" by Taylor Swift) to authors (letting the mind wander and then writing down those thoughts is a major element of modernists like James Joyce) to film. *Alice* has been adapted into a Disney movie and inspired phrases like "mad tea party" and "down the rabbit hole."

# ROBERT LOUIS STEVENSON

Set a Course for Adventure

Robert Louis Stevenson was one of the primary entertainers of the growing middle and lower classes in late nineteenth-century England. He wrote wide-eyed, highly descriptive tales of high adventure and the unbelievable, and two of his most notable books, *Treasure Island* and *Strange Case of Dr. Jekyll and Mr. Hyde*, provided the world with the popular perception of pirates and the archetypes of horror, respectively.

## WANDERLUST

Born in Scotland in 1850, Stevenson wrote tales of adventure because he traveled the world in search of adventure. Both his wanderlust and his desire to write, which informed each other, were born of a desire to escape the dreary but stable future laid out in front of him: to go into the family business of lighthouse design. Stevenson even enrolled at Edinburgh University at seventeen to study engineering in preparation before switching to the more word-based discipline of law. During summer breaks, he'd vacation in France in order to hang around with lawyers and painters. The travel and the interesting people were more educational than the law—despite graduating with a legal degree in 1875, Stevenson never practiced and pursued travel and writing in equal parts instead.

# A MAN OF THE WORLD

Travelogues were an extremely popular book genre in Stevenson's era, just as travel TV shows are popular in the 2000s. Humans just seem to love to get a glimpse of distant lands and cultures, and in the 1870s, when photography was still in its infancy, reading about them was about the only way to do it. Stevenson took advantage of the public hunger for travelogues with his first book, *An Inland Voyage* (1878), which recounts a canoeing trip down the Oise River through Belgium and France. And while most travelogues of the time were dry, fact-based accounts of a journey, Stevenson told his with flair and flourish. He also had a unique hook—his story wasn't about just a trip on a boat; it was a trip on a tiny canoe. He's the narrator, but he writes as if the book were a novel with a first-person point of view. In *An Inland Voyage* and the follow-up *Travels with a Donkey in the Cévennes* (again, he had a hook), Stevenson entertainingly blurred the lines between narrative fiction and journalism.

Based on the success of his two nonfiction books, Stevenson journeyed all the way over to fiction, and to America. In 1878, he'd married an American woman named Fanny Osbourne, and they honeymooned in, of all places, an abandoned silver mine in northern California. The purpose of the visit was twofold—Stevenson likely had an undiagnosed case of tuberculosis, and he sought out warm climates to improve his health. While living in the United States, hemorrhaging lungs confined him to a bed for months at a time, leaving him little to do but write. He was bedridden when he wrote two classic novels: *Treasure Island* (published in 1883) and *Strange Case of Dr. Jekyll and Mr. Hyde* (1886).

# BEWARE, PIRATES

*Treasure Island* is the prototypical pirate adventure story. Truly scary individuals looting ships on the high seas, terrorizing the British Navy at that very time, came to life from the safe distance of pages, where Victorian audiences could explore without getting too close. Ironically, pirates became heroic and attractive, such was how Stevenson rendered, and romanticized, them. All of the details modern audiences associate with pirates come from *Treasure Island*, from singing songs about rum to peg legs to pet parrots to hidden treasure maps to black marks to treasure chests.

In a bit of adorable inspiration, Stevenson got the idea when he drew a treasure map for his twelve-year-old stepson. He embellished a story to go along with the map, and that story was serialized in the young-reader periodical *Young Folks* from October 1881 to January 1882. It was extremely popular among the readers, but became a bestseller when it was published as a book in 1882. It became one of the bestselling books—of any kind—of the decade.

# THE MONSTER WITHIN

Another one of Stevenson's bestselling books of the 1880s, although completely different and for a totally different audience, was *Strange Case of Dr. Jekyll and Mr. Hyde*. On its surface a particularly thrilling and spooky tale about a scientist who takes a potion that allows him to have split personalities—one good and one evil—the novella has some symbolic meanings and social commentary about the different personalities living inside us all and how our bad sides can sabotage our good sides. (A perfectly Victorian sentiment.) One of the most famous and simple tales, it's been adapted for the stage, made into a film more than 100 times, and satirized and referenced often.

## Literary Lessons

One of Stevenson's most enduring and popular books was almost lost forever. Right after Stevenson completed his first draft of *Strange Case of Dr. Jekyll and Mr. Hyde*, his wife, Fanny, read it and hated it so much that she threw it in a fire. Stevenson didn't raise much of a fuss. He was so happy with the book (which he personally considered his finest work) that he was able to rewrite it in just three days.

# FOR CHILDREN?

Stevenson's works were very approachable and easy to read, designed to appeal to a broad audience. That's in part why today his books, particularly *Treasure Island*, are most often read by children. He also wrote Victorian novels: Characters are very clearly good or evil, and the good guys always win out through the Victorian values of hard work and perseverance. Be that as it may, Stevenson didn't write inside of a Victorian vacuum—his stories of distant adventure like *Treasure Island* owe a lot to Jonathan Swift and Daniel Defoe (at least plot-wise), and *Dr. Jekyll and Mr. Hyde* is as dark, gloomy, and frightening as anything produced in the gothic romantic era.

# TAKE IT EASY

Forever in search of warmer climates to ease his lung disease, Stevenson and his family ventured to the Pacific Islands in 1888. The first stop was Hawaii (where he became a guest at the court of King Kalakaua), before settling in 1889 in Samoa, where they built a house. The islands improved his health somewhat, enough for him to write Pacific Islands–set works, such as *The Wrecker, The Ebb-Tide*, and *Island Nights' Entertainments*. They were casual, laid-back works describing daily life, not so much grand adventure. They were more personal and showed off his storytelling abilities beyond all the trappings of pirates and monsters. Stevenson died of a stroke in 1894. Most of his works remain in print, and were a major source of inspiration for writers like Rudyard Kipling and J.M. Barrie in particular.

# RUDYARD KIPLING

Welcome to the *Jungle*

While a native English speaker and born to English parents, Rudyard Kipling is among the first major English authors to emerge in the wake of British imperialism and colonialism. That point of view—and an unapologetic stance on England's might and rightness—is very much reflected in his work, although today he's most remembered for creating children's stories, particularly *The Jungle Book*.

## EARLY LIFE

Rudyard Kipling was born in Bombay, in 1865, where his father was the principal of the Sir Jamsetjee Jeejebhoy School of Art. Foreshadowing the very East versus West, or native versus colonial issues his son would one day address in his works, John Lockwood Kipling had settled on the subcontinent in the first place to restore and encourage native Indian art and architecture, and defend it against British colonialists who aimed to steal, sell, or exploit Indian art and artists. In 1871, six-year-old Rudyard Kipling was sent back to his parents' England for his education (where he lived in a boarding house that he called "The House of Desolation" because the landlady and her son bullied and abused him).

He honed his skills writing and editing school newspapers, but his father's career as an art curator and activist meant there wasn't money for him to attend college. So in 1882, Kipling returned to India and entered the workforce, serving as assistant editor of an English newspaper in Lahore called the *Civil and Military Gazette*. Meanwhile, he started writing poems and adventure stories for some of the dozens of magazines and pulp collections published in England. Kipling got his stories published so often that he thought he could forge a career as a more legitimate writer back in England, and so he headed back in 1889.

He was right. His first collection of stories, *Plain Tales from the Hills*—highly descriptive and captivating tales of exotic India, but written with the middle-class, white English audience in mind—enraptured audiences. Readers enjoyed the playful rhymes, dialogue written in accents, and imperialism-affirming themes of his work. By 1890, Kipling was a literary superstar, as famous and loved in his own time among the English as Charles Dickens was. Ironically, he spent very little of his life *in* England—his youth was spent in India, and for much of his adult life he lived in Vermont with his American wife.

# FROM THE JUNGLES OF VERMONT

While in Vermont, Kipling wrote his most popular and enduring works, *The Jungle Book* (1894) and the creatively titled *The Second Jungle Book* (1895). Kipling structured them to read like ancient folk tales, although they bear a lot of his own creative invention—like the imperialistic style of the day, Kipling took something Indian and Anglicized it. Kipling said that his inspiration was a story he'd heard as a young boy in India about a South African lion hunter who lived among lions and helped them form an alliance against villainous baboons—which certainly sounds like Kipling's loosely connected *Jungle Book* stories about Mowgli, the child raised by wolves who enjoys and endures alliances and rivalries against a number of different animals. The stories also bear resemblance to the *Jataka* tales of India, which date to the fourth century B.C.

## Quotable Voices

"The Law of the Jungle, which never orders anything without a reason, forbids every beast to eat Man except when he is killing to show his children how to kill, and then he must hunt outside the hunting grounds of his pack or tribe. The real reason for this is that man-killing means, sooner or later, the arrival of white men on elephants, with guns, and hundreds of brown men with gongs and rockets and torches. Then everybody in the jungle suffers."

—*The Jungle Book*

In 1896, Kipling returned to England, and wrote a vivid adventure novel about the high seas: *Captains Courageous*. Like Kipling's other works, it can be enjoyed on more than one level. At its surface, the novel is about Harvey Cheyne Jr., a spoiled brat who falls overboard on a long sea journey and joins the crew of the fishing boat that rescues him. In doing so, he becomes a self-made man. While that's a formulaic and inspiring story, it really serves to reinforce Kipling's cheerleading of Englishness: Harvey is a self-made man because that's an English value, and being cunning and brave is how the English at the time wanted to see themselves; and that what England was doing around the world wasn't money- or power-driven but done out of a calling to spread English values.

# WHAT A BOER

In 1901, Kipling wrote *Kim*, a mature, very Victorian novel and a serious attempt to explain the complicated politics that informed contemporary Anglo-Indian relations. It's about an Irish orphan boy named Kim who grows up homeless in Lahore (a city in India at the time, but which today is in Pakistan), only to be recruited by his dead father's old army regiment to spy on Russia, on behalf of England, on the Indian border.

Kipling's late-career poetry was also largely about nationalism and international politics, despite an England that had shifted politically to the left and away from the English pride of the Victorian era. His voice was one of jingoism and imperialism, and was tied to political philosophies that had led England into the bloody Boer War, as well as World War I. Nevertheless, he was awarded the Nobel Prize for Literature in 1907.

Most of Kipling's works are entrenched in their cultural climate, and little of his work is read today outside of *The Jungle Book*, most famous because of its many adaptations to film. But its themes, particularly about the conflict between man's base needs and his need to civilize himself and others, are highly representative of Victorian fiction. At any rate, he added to the canon the rich imagery of India and the East, a refreshing contrast to the filthy London streets or pastoral landscapes that dominated the form.

# OSCAR WILDE

For Art's Sake

As versatile as Shakespeare, as famous as Dickens, and as witty as Jonathan Swift, Oscar Wilde possessed the definitive British wit of the late Victorian age and the early modern age, both of which he was equally at home in and took great delight in skewering. Both a populist and an intellectual, Wilde wrote multiple major plays (comedies, tragedies, and histories), a single classic impressionistic novel (*The Picture of Dorian Gray*), poetry, children's stories, critical essays, and social commentary, and developed truly progressive notions about the meaning and purpose of art itself.

## MENTORS AND MODERNISM

Oscar Wilde was born in Dublin, Ireland, but educated at Oxford, where he studied with art historians John Ruskin and Walter Pater. Through those mentors, Wilde developed his own artistic thesis that would become one of the tenets for all of modernism: Art should be created for art's sake. Art should exist on its own plane, free of both judgment and purpose. Society had evolved, Wilde believed, to the point where art didn't really need to say anything or provide any kind of lesson or purpose. Wilde didn't think that art should by its nature be superficial (even his own breezy comic plays contain brutal satire of the upper classes), just that art should be its own thing, and artists needn't consider any ethical concerns before making it.

This idea of "art for the sake of art" informed Wilde's entire creative life, as did his Irish background and the social problems of the era. The gap between the rich and the poor grew ever wider in the late nineteenth century—from the millions who lived in poverty despite working endlessly in factories and mills to the high classes who lived in luxury and did little more than pass judgment on what was "proper." Wilde himself was from a working-class Irish family, and yet presented himself to London from 1879 onward as a character—a bon vivant and a bit of a dandy, witty, fashionable, chatty, and catty. Wilde became a known figure in high society, but as an object of scorn—by pretending to be frivolous, he mocked the upper crust to their faces.

Wilde didn't care much for the realism dominating literature in his era because it wasn't in his aesthetic palate. He didn't care much for holding up a mirror to society or the human psyche. Instead, he wanted to create structured stage worlds that were the vehicle for his funny, grammatically agile, often paradoxical quips delivered as dialogue. (Art for the sake of art, indeed.) His 1892 play *Lady Windermere's Fan* established this template. Like many of his plays, the plot itself is a conventional, predictable combination of a farce and comedy of manners involving mistaken identities and snobs getting knocked down a peg. Ironically enjoyed by snobs—fashionable Victorian society—*Lady Windermere's Fan* earned Wilde a curtain call on opening night and ran for 156 performances. More importantly, Wilde was credited with reviving the English stage comedy, dormant since the era of Richard Sheridan in the 1770s.

# EXTREMELY IMPORTANT

In 1895, *The Importance of Being Earnest* debuted. Perhaps the most famous stage comedy of all time, the play about mistaken identity and grown men shirking their social responsibility by creating a fake relative and getting involved in a scheme about unknown parentage may seem light, but it's highly pointed. Wilde didn't think art needed to serve a purpose, but his work almost always did. Even *Importance* attacks middle-class superficiality and commercialism. The point of *Importance* is that being respectable and proper leads to a boring, joyless life.

## Quotable Voices

"I hope you have not been leading a double life, pretending to be wicked and being good all the time. That would be hypocrisy."

—*The Importance of Being Earnest*

Wilde often wrote about the need for free expression, perhaps because even in spite of his actions to loosen up society, he had to live much of his life in secret. *The Importance of Being Earnest* and his novel *The Picture of Dorian Gray* are about secret-keeping and contain coded messages. Wilde himself lived a double life—married with two children, he was a homosexual forced to stay in the closet— much like the portrait of Dorian Gray that tragically ages while the real Dorian puts on a brave, fake face.

# GROSS INDECENCY

The society Wilde wanted to be a part of ultimately turned against him because they didn't like who he was or what he had to say. Wilde was Irish, and an outspoken socialist—an affront in every possible way to the Victorian system. In 1895, the Marquess of Queensberry accused Wilde of "posing" as a homosexual, as Wilde had been involved with his son, Lord Alfred Douglas. Wilde, ever the showman and wit, made the decision to sue him for libel. It was very easy to prove Wilde was a homosexual—details of his affairs were discovered and he was charged under the 1885 "gross indecency act" that made homosexuality a crime. He served two years in a hard labor camp from 1895 to 1897.

## Quotable Voices

"Society, as we have constituted it, will have no place for me, has none to offer; but Nature, whose sweet rains fall on unjust and just alike, will have clefts in the rocks where I may hide, and secret valleys in whose silence I may weep undisturbed. She will hang the night with stars so that I may walk abroad in the darkness without stumbling, and send the wind over my footprints so that none may track me to my hurt: she will cleanse me in great waters, and with bitter herbs make me whole."

—*De Profundis*

While he was in prison, Wilde wrote critical essays and letters on political and social matters. His final work, *The Ballad of Reading Gaol*, was written after his release. Published in 1898 and credited to "C.3.3," his cell number at Reading Gaol, the ballad tells the story of a man condemned to death for murdering his wife. It's the most realistically detailed thing Wilde would ever write, especially in terms of the sadness and guilt it conveys.

Similarly, Wilde eluded attention after his prison release. He wandered Europe for three and a half years under an assumed name, Sebastian Melmoth, and died bankrupt in a Paris hotel on November 30, 1900.

# THOMAS HARDY

Going Backward to Go Forward

Thomas Hardy wrote some of the most popular and enduring Victorian novels. Similar to Dickens and Austen but without the happy endings, Hardy primarily wrote about rural England in the late nineteenth century. Hardy believed that most country people were unhappy and suffered endlessly due to the rise of modernity. The march of technology threatened to eliminate the ideal rural way of life, thereby deeply damaging the souls of men. Hardy considered himself primarily a poet, and his poems also echoed the failings of society and the drain-circling British culture.

## AN ARCHITECTURAL APPROACH

Hardy was born in 1840 in the idyllic Dorset village of Upper Bockhampton. The son of a builder and a cook, Hardy spent most of his childhood exploring the outdoors that he would one day idealize in his fiction. He also studied Latin and French at a school set up by the Church of England for poor children such as himself. He most enjoyed literature, particularly Greek and Roman classics, Shakespeare, Alexandre Dumas, and epic stories of adventure and romance.

Unable to attend a major university because his family couldn't afford it, Hardy left school in 1856 to apprentice for an architect who specialized in church restoration. After discovering the poetry of a local schoolteacher named William Barnes, Hardy began writing odes to rural life, like Barnes, in the local Dorset dialect. While restoring a church, Hardy met a Cambridge-educated son of a vicar who introduced him to contemporary English literature, such as the poetry of Alfred, Lord Tennyson, and Charles Darwin's *On the Origin of Species*. That's when Hardy decided to move to London (landing another job with an architect to pay the bills), where he surrounded himself with art and culture: He attended plays, went to museums, and saw Charles Dickens lecture.

In 1865, Hardy entered a writing contest with a short story called "How I Built Myself a House"—and he won. Yet he still turned to poetry to spill his heart out onto the page. A crisis of faith led him to reject Christianity and he instead embraced the concepts that would define his work. He was very skeptical of technological progress, because it stifled individuality and led to human misery.

Hardy continued to work for architects while he wrote and published novels to little notice, such as:

- *The Poor Man and the Lady*
- *Desperate Remedies*
- *Under the Greenwood Tree*
- *A Pair of Blue Eyes*

Finally, in 1874, he broke through with *Far from the Madding Crowd*. The book was set in a fictional part of southwest England he called Wessex, a pastoral area struck by both financial decline and a disconnect with nature due to the advancement of industry and modernity. Those problems eventually and inevitably lead to misery for the characters. *Far from the Madding Crowd* was a publishing success for Hardy, enough so that he was able to give up architecture and devote himself full time to writing. With his windfall from sales of *Far from the Madding Crowd,* Hardy and his wife moved into a riverfront house in the village of Sturminster Newton. That town is in Dorset, the real-life Wessex, although it was not in as much decline or in danger of losing its identity as other areas of Dorset. Hardy later wrote that his time in Sturminster Newton was the happiest time in his life.

## Quotable Voices

"The beauty or ugliness of a character lay not only in its achievements, but in its aims and impulses; its true history lay, not among things done, but among things willed."

—*Tess of the d'Urbervilles*

# A NOVEL APPROACH

Hardy's novel *Tess of the d'Urbervilles* caused a bit of a scandal when it was released in 1891. Both gloomy and sexual, it did not follow the format of the usual Victorian novel. The villain was a nasty aristocrat for one, and he proceeded to seduce and have his way with the beautiful, young, and innocent Tess. Hardy was forced to tone down the sexual content and immorality in the novel so it could be published. He had to do the same thing in 1895 for the release of the also sexually suggestive *Jude the Obscure*. So annoyed by having to change his novels for them to see the light of day—a form he only took up because he couldn't make a living at writing poetry—Hardy announced in 1898 that he was done with prose entirely and would return to verse. He changed formats, but still situated his work in the country, and, in 1898, he released a compilation of older poems called *Wessex Poems*. Hardy kept to his promise, writing about 1,000 poems until his death thirty years later. One major, and majorly ambitious, work during the latter years of Hardy's life was the *The Dynasts*, a series of three plays (consisting of 130 scenes) about the Napoleonic Wars that rocked Europe between 1803 and 1815. Again, Hardy kept to his promise. The plays are written in verse.

# Chapter 6

# The Modernist Movement

All of the social change, technological progress, and better understanding of the self felt pointless after the death and destruction of World War I. Writers wondered if attempts to understand humanity were even worth it. Instead, the adherents of what would come to be called modernism rallied by questioning absolutely everything, even the very tools of literature.

There's a starkness to modernism, as it strips away a lot of the decoration and flourishes of previous literary movements. Modernist writers found their world to be cold, industrial, and alienating. It follows that the old methods of storytelling didn't work for them, so modernists created new narrative forms.

Virginia Woolf mixed dream states with stories told out of order. James Joyce played with language and stream of consciousness so intensely that sometimes his works are inscrutable. In other authors' books, narrators were either unreliable or part of the story they were telling. Reality itself was untrustworthy, and so was the fragmented reality of modernist fiction, more often than not written in the first person, which amazingly hadn't been attempted much before the twentieth century.

In modernist literature, characters became symbolic archetypes of philosophies, intended to be satirized or examined. And at the end of the book, there was no happy ending … if there even *was* an ending. The work became about the work itself. The only holdover from romantic poetry was that the author was to be celebrated for his or her singular and unique point of view.

# WILLIAM BUTLER YEATS

The Diamond of the Emerald Isle

Ireland's most important poet, William Butler Yeats was born in Sandymount, just outside of Dublin, in 1865. His mother was from a wealthy merchant family and his father was a painter. The family lived on a large country home in a beautiful pastoral setting, the kind of beautiful Irish countryside that poets like Yeats would forever try to do justice. When he was a child, the family moved to England to advance John Yeats's painting career, and William had a hard time adjusting from home schooling and country life to formal schooling in urban London. Fortunately, the brood returned to Dublin when Yeats turned fifteen; he continued to go to school, but spent most of his time hanging out at his father's art studio, a gathering place for Dublin's writers and artists. That's where Yeats first found encouragement to write poetry; by the time he was twenty, his first collection of Ireland-centric poetry had been published in the *Dublin University Review*.

## Quotable Voices

"O what fine thought we had because we thought
That the worst rogues and rascals had died out.
All teeth were drawn, all ancient tricks unlearned,
And a great army but a showy thing;
What matter that no cannon had been turned
Into a ploughshare? Parliament and king
Thought that unless a little powder burned
The trumpeters might burst with trumpeting
And yet it lack all glory;"

—"Nineteen Hundred and Nineteen"

Yeats was highly influenced by the sprawling, emotional poetry of Percy Bysshe Shelley and William Blake, but also the careful cultivation employed by older poets like Edmund Spenser—all informed his passion for writing love poems. In 1887, he returned to London, for it had a larger literary scene than Dublin. There he joined a collective called the Rhymers' Club, which consisted, not surprisingly, of poets who got together at taverns to read their verse.

Because he comes from the Irish tradition, Yeats's work is often misconstrued as mystical and lofty, but it was actually quite gritty and engaged. Because he understood both Irish literary forms and distinctly British ones, he's an icon in both worlds and bridged the gap between Irish literature and English literature. But Yeats is mostly—and passionately—associated with Ireland. His work was a point of Irish national pride, and was often invoked in the Irish independence movement in the 1910s and 1920s, as he deftly compared the stifling of Irish art to the oppression of Ireland itself. As he wrote in "September 1913":

"Romantic Ireland's dead and gone, / It's with O'Leary in the grave."

He'd touch on the theme of independence again in "Easter, 1916," a poem about the Easter Rising, an unsuccessful attempt by Irish leaders to expel English authorities. Yeats's work makes it clear that his sensitive, poet-type personality is at odds with his desire for a free Ireland—he questions if freedom is worth it, if it's born of violence. "Nineteen Hundred and Nineteen," about the beginnings of the Anglo-Irish War (which would ultimately end in 1921 with an independent Ireland), manages to be both a grand defense of art as well as a case against violence, all while acknowledging in a modernist kind of way that humans have both the capacity, if not the need, for both art *and* violence.

# IRELAND'S POET

Ireland did get its independence, and through the blood and struggle that Yeats feared. He put those romantic-styled feelings of anguish to page, and doing so became the leading poet of the time, instilling pride in his countrymen. Yeats became the most famous poet in Irish history despite his discomfort with violence.

Yeats did much to advance the art and culture of Ireland. In 1904, he cofounded the Irish National Theatre Society, and the society opened the Abbey Theatre, which became the National Theatre of Ireland. With his sister Elizabeth Yeats, he founded Cuala Press, a publishing company (that began with a single hand press) devoted to Irish authors. Cuala printed works by Irish luminaries such as Lady Gregory, John Millington Synge, and Yeats himself. Yeats, his press, and his theater sparked the Irish Literary Revival, a movement calling for more homegrown literature.

## Quotable Voices

"O sages standing in God's holy fire
As in the gold mosaic of a wall,
Come from the holy fire, perne in a gyre,
And be the singing-masters of my soul.
Consume my heart away; sick with desire
And fastened to a dying animal
It knows not what it is; and gather me
Into the artifice of eternity."

—"Sailing to Byzantium"

In 1923, less than two years after Ireland became a free state, Yeats became the first Irish national to receive the Nobel Prize for Literature. The committee honored the poet for his "inspired poetry, which in a highly artistic form gives expression to the spirit of a whole nation."

# T.S. ELIOT

Going to *Waste*

T.S. Eliot was of that rare breed of British writer who's actually . . .
American. He was born in St. Louis in 1888, but transformed himself
into his own image of a British person, and then contributed to the
British literary tradition to such an extent that he's claimed by the
British canon.

## HEADING EAST

Thomas Stearns Eliot came from a wealthy Midwestern family, and
slowly began to make his way east to England by first matriculating
at Harvard in 1906, where he finished an undergraduate degree in
three years. Eliot's mother was a poet and instilled a love of the form
in him. Classical poetry was among the three things he studied at the
Ivy League institution, along with philosophy and literary criticism.
All three would deeply inform his life's work. During his study of
classical poetry, he'd try to emulate nineteenth-century French symbolist poets such as Charles Baudelaire and Arthur Rimbaud. Eliot's
modernist poetry can be described as a combination of the French
poets' use of precise symbolism and images presented dreamily and
sensually, then combined with the psychological detail and ironic
detachment pioneered by French symbolist poet Jules Laforgue.

After a year at the Sorbonne in Paris, Eliot returned to Harvard
for postgraduate work in Sanskrit, then back to Europe, where he
got stuck when World War I broke out. It was for the best, sort of:
He married a British woman, Vivienne Haigh-Wood, and took a job

as an analyst of foreign documents at Lloyds Bank in London (his mastery of foreign languages landed him the gig). He'd toil away at the job for ten years, which certainly contributed to the feelings of unease and dissatisfaction inherent in his poetry, as would his unhappy marriage to Haigh-Wood, who spent years in and out of mental institutions.

## PULLING FROM THE PAST

During this time period, Eliot found great support in a group of expatriate American writers who were so politically liberal and so artistically experimental that they left the United States for Europe. Other members of the group included:

- Gertrude Stein
- F. Scott Fitzgerald
- Ernest Hemingway
- Ezra Pound

Pound thought Eliot's sensibility and goals—to revolutionize poetry in terms of both technique and subject matter—were similar to his own. Pound helped Eliot get his first major work—"The Love Song of J. Alfred Prufrock"—into *Poetry* magazine in 1915. In pitching Eliot to *Poetry* editor Harriet Monroe, Pound boasted that Eliot was especially impressive because he hadn't trained in any one discipline, and hadn't even been writing for all that long. Pound wrote:

"He actually trained himself and modernized himself on his own."

"The Love Song of J. Alfred Prufrock," one of Eliot's most famous, would use the symbolism Eliot learned from his influences, along with the bizarre metaphors that could have come from a metaphysical poet like John Donne, to express the disillusionment that was epidemic among his generation. Life felt like a bit of a sad fraud to Eliot and his brethren, particularly after the death and destruction of World War I and the imposed, false morality of the Victorian era.

## Quotable Voices

"And would it have been worth it, after all,
Would it have been worth while,
After the sunsets and the dooryards and the sprinkled streets,
After the novels, after the teacups, after the skirts that trail along the floor—
And this, and so much more?—"

—"The Love Song of J. Alfred Prufrock"

# THINKING IT THROUGH

One thing Eliot does in his early work is apply the relatively new science of psychology to poetry. Literature had always been about exploring the why and how of human nature, and thanks to pioneers like Carl Jung and Sigmund Freud, in the early twentieth century writers had this lively scientific tool of analysis in their arsenal. Rationality mixed with emotion while delving into the subconscious mind is definitively modernist, and Eliot explores the nuances of human thought and feelings with both grace and wit.

Thanks to "Prufrock," Eliot's reputation grew over the next few years, and in 1919 he published a collection called *Poems*. A standout of the collection was a poem titled "Gerontion," which was received as more psychologically real than anything published in English to that point. It was a stream-of-consciousness interior monologue that presented the subject's diversions and dark thoughts, warts and all. And the poem lost none of its vitality even though it was written in the now centuries-old poetic structure of blank verse.

## Quotable Voices

"History has many cunning passages, contrived corridors and issues."

—"Gerontion"

# A TOWERING ACHIEVEMENT

In 1922, Eliot published "The Waste Land," a poem that featured a collection of dramatic scenes based on moments Eliot pulled from his own life. Eliot wrote this work after suffering a nervous breakdown after the death of his father and experiencing the end of his marriage, so there's a hopelessness and sadness in the work. On a grander scale, this work is also an intricate, emotionally intense dissertation on twentieth-century disillusionment, but the scores of literary references make it feel more at home with classical works while the jazz-like, syncopated beats frame the "The Waste Land" squarely in the 1920s. Influential critic Edmund Wilson wrote an essay proclaiming it one of the most important poems of the twentieth century.

"A heap of broken images, where the sun beats,
And the dead tree gives no shelter, the cricket no relief,
And the dry stone no sound of water. Only
There is shadow under this red rock,
(Come in under the shadow of this red rock),
And I will show you something different from either
Your shadow at morning striding behind you
Or your shadow at evening rising to meet you;
I will show you fear in a handful of dust."

—"The Waste Land"

# SWITCHING GEARS

Eliot was a forward thinker and he kept moving forward. In the late 1920s, he joined the Church of England and suddenly his work was concerned almost entirely with Christianity and conservative politics, largely abandoning the ideals of his early career. In 1930, Eliot announced that he was

"a classicist in literature, royalist in politics, and Anglo-Catholic in religion."

His poems of the time include "Journey of the Magi" (1927) and the six-part epic *Ash Wednesday* (1930). The rare exception: On a lark he wrote a book of verse for children called *Old Possum's Book of Practical Cats*. It would later serve as the very unlikely inspiration for Andrew Lloyd Webber's musical *Cats*.

Mostly Eliot had moved on to plays, in which he attempted to combine the crisp dialogue of the comedies of early twentieth-century English playwright Noel Coward with religious themes and classical plots. Eliot's blank verse drama *The Family Reunion*, for example, is based on *The Eumenides,* the third and final part of ancient Greek playwright Aeschylus's trilogy called *The Oresteia.* Eliot mostly keeps intact the source material's plot—a once admirable man wrestles with his guilt over a murder, and whether or not he even deserves to be redeemed. Eliot changed the setting from ancient Greece to a manor home in 1930s England.

Playwriting and political writing occupied most of the rest of Eliot's life. He was awarded the Nobel Prize for Literature in 1948 and died in 1965.

# D.H. LAWRENCE

Love Gone Wrong

Up until the late nineteenth century, nearly every major English author or poet of note had been born into a family of privilege. Whether their families were members of the aristocracy or merely extremely wealthy, these writers had all the advantageous resources they'd need to pursue a career in the arts, such as an education at Oxford or Cambridge as well as the leisure time needed to hone their craft. D.H. Lawrence represents a major break from that tradition.

Born in the rural coal-mining community of Eastwood, Nottinghamshire, in 1885, David Herbert Lawrence was the son of two working parents: a coal miner and a lace maker. Lawrence's parents had come from wealthy families but by the time they had married, they had lost most of their fortune, but not their literary instincts. Lawrence's mother was formally educated and encouraged the future author to rise above his station in life, which he did.

Lawrence was among the first post–industrial age writers to be truly working class, writing about and for an underserved population: the masses of people who were like him. That said, Lawrence was from the "anything goes" school when it came to his fiction. Because Lawrence wrote about real people as realistically as he could, his writing tended to be quite salacious as he wrote emotionally honest and psychologically complex accounts of relationships, sexuality, and a class system on its last legs.

# ART IMITATES LIFE,
# LIFE IMITATES ART

After graduating from the high school he attended on scholarship, Lawrence attended University College, Nottingham (on scholarship) and in 1906 won a short-story competition for "An Enjoyable Christmas: A Prelude," which he entered under the name of his friend, Jessie Chambers, so he could submit multiple stories. Chambers would be an early advocate for Lawrence's work, helping him publish poems in the *English Review* and recommending his first novel, *The White Peacock*, to a publisher in 1911. Set in Lawrence's hometown of Eastwood, *The White Peacock* lays out the Lawrence template: the madness of a society in which working-class people struggle to get by financially and can't marry for love outside of their social class, resulting in many unhappy marriages.

Star-crossed, class-mismatched lovers would recur in Lawrence's novels, as well as in his own life. Around the time *The White Peacock* was published, he fell in love with a German aristocrat named Frieda Weekley, a mother of three children who had been married before. But in the eyes of London society that Weekley was at home in, Lawrence was just some son of a coal miner. And so, society rejected their relationship. Nevertheless, they eloped to Germany.

Lawrence wrote passionately of the abilities of love (and sex) to naturally motivate man to action in an attempt to pursue what's wanted within and beyond the artificial constraints of society. Lawrence wanted his work to both call out and bring down the oppressive—and falsely constructed—cultural norms of the early twentieth century. He once said:

"If there weren't so many lies in the world ... I wouldn't write at all."

He wrote about those big themes on a personal level, showing how they affect love, marriage, and family relationships.

# COURTING CONTROVERSY

While living with Weekley in Italy in 1913, Lawrence published *Sons and Lovers*. In this work, the once wealthy widow Gertrude Morel marries down, to a coal miner, and the pressures placed on them by polite society's disapproval makes it an unhappy marriage, made worse by the fact that they don't have much money. Gertrude seeks comfort by becoming unhealthily attached to her grown sons, first William, who dies, then Paul, who ultimately rejects true love to spend his life with his mother. *Sons and Lovers* is an example of the growing trend of modernism in that the book does not have a happy ending, or even a resolved one: Paul no longer has love, and then Gertrude dies. Other modernist themes include Lawrence's realistically rendered relationships—quirks and all—including the borderline Oedipal arrangement, as well as the pervading idea that the English social system is useless, outdated, makes people miserable, and is degrading.

*Sons and Lovers* sold well enough that Lawrence began to write full time and traveled back and forth between his home country and Italy (which he found to be far more reasonable and more libertine than stuffy old England). He started to write another novel about romance, sex, and relationships that got so long that he split it into two novels. The first half, *The Rainbow*, was published in 1915, but due to some graphic sex scenes, it was banned in England for obscenity and all the copies were confiscated and burned. That abruptly interrupted any financial or artistic success Lawrence was enjoying.

Then, the outbreak of World War I kept Lawrence from returning to Italy, so he moved to Cornwall. But once there, authorities kicked him out of the coastal town—he was considered a security risk because his wife was German.

## FORBIDDEN LOVE

Lawrence wrote in short bursts while he and Weekley moved around through various friends' homes in England until the end of the war. Then they moved to Italy and Lawrence published *Women in Love* in 1920. The second half of *The Rainbow*, *Women in Love* is about two women who fall in love with two men and hang out in artist salons and underground clubs in London. A thoroughly modernist novel, it's really a look at how globalization, industrialization, and war have changed interpersonal relationships in that they've created personal isolation, distance, and an inability to relate. It also ends ominously, with an attempted murder and successful suicide.

## THE *LOVER*

After spending much of the 1920s traveling and resting in warm climates to treat his worsening tuberculosis, Lawrence published *Lady Chatterley's Lover* in 1928—or at least he tried to. The novel was accepted for publication in Italy, but like *The Rainbow*, was banned in England. It's the story of a forbidden relationship between the aristocratic Lady Chatterley and her groundskeeper. Sexually explicit to the point of being sexually graphic, the book's sexuality isn't necessarily gratuitous or titillating—it's a huge part of the plot and characters' motivations. Lord Chatterley was paralyzed in World War I and is impotent, which is why Lady Chatterley seeks out the affair. That forthrightness alone understandably raised eyebrows, as did the long, detailed love scenes. Realism as it applied to sex scandalized the nation's upper crust (the lower classes didn't much care) who were still mired in the Victorian mores of not talking about anything and repressing anything biological or untoward.

The novel was just too much for its time. *Lady Chatterley's Lover* was banned in the United States until 1959 and England until 1960. In the UK a jury found Penguin Books not guilty of violating Britain's Obscene Publications Act and finally allowed it to be published. The trial was a turning point in freedom of expression, a death knell for censorship, and the true opening of sexual discussions in polite society and in popular culture. For better or for worse, sexual themes in books, movies, and television began with D.H. Lawrence.

Lawrence didn't live long enough to see the mainstream acceptance of the sexual themes of which he wrote extensively. Tuberculosis claimed his life in 1930, at age forty-four. Still caught up in the *Lady Chatterley* controversy, Lawrence died in a state of disrespect, his reputation as an author in jeopardy due to the pervading idea that he'd given up literature to write pornography.

# E.M. FORSTER

Where Nature Meets Human Nature

E.M. Forster's life straddles a unique timespan. Born in 1879 and dying in 1970, Forster witnessed firsthand and wrote about the late Victorian era, as well as both World Wars, postwar Britain, and even the rise of film. Forster was a guiding hand of English literature, particularly the novel, from the staid nineteenth century to the freewheeling if neurotic twentieth century. E.M. Forster dominated the world of English novels in the first two decades of the twentieth century. His stories were so universal and compelling—but rendered in such attractive, ornate detail and driven by palpable salaciousness—that it's no surprise that those same books (*A Room with a View*, *Howards End*, and *A Passage to India*) also came to dominate highbrow film in the final two decades of the twentieth century.

## LOOKING TO ITALY

After suffering through a childhood education that he didn't feel was academically rigorous enough, Forster enrolled in Cambridge, and upon graduating received an inheritance from an aunt. That allowed him to travel extensively through Italy and Greece, where he could study the cultures he'd read about and been attracted to.

While Forster didn't quite call for an outright rejection of Victorian customs and modern conveniences in favor of an embrace of nature (an opinion set forth by, among others, contemporaries like Thomas Hardy), he raised the question that the individual and his or her uniqueness was being swallowed up by the onslaught of industrialism. Forster believed in the importance and healthiness of skepticism to question rapid change. To that end, his work often compared the ideals of the relatively freewheeling and philosophically experimental ancient Greece and Rome to the artificially strait-laced values of nineteenth-century Europe. To Forster, England (the people and the climate) was dull, stratified, and cold. The Mediterranean, however, was just as romantic, beautiful, and warm as he'd imagined. It's no surprise that his novels frequently involve English people exploring Italy or that he set his first novel, *Where Angels Fear to Tread* (1905), in Tuscany.

Forster did believe that one of the elements of happiness involved some kind of contact with nature, picking up on a theme passed down by the romantics. To this he added in the importance of imagination and being progressive. In other words, Forster called for balance between the natural and the artificial, and the old and the new, which he felt Italy was handling quite well by accepting industrialization but maintaining its romance and history. England, however, lacked that balance, and Forster found it repressed by social divisions and rules. His home country was hung up on social divisions and industrialization at the expense of the heart and the mind. His novel *The Longest Journey* (1907) is about a Cambridge-educated young man named Rickie Elliott who takes a teaching job, which curtails his ambition of becoming a writer. Rickie abandons his job and shunning family to care for his alcoholic half-brother, but ultimately dies in trying to save his troubled relative. In short, society made it impossible for him to follow both social constructs and his heart.

While embracing modernity, Forster also called for social change as a way to truly embrace that modernity and a sense of balance. He wrote about women in a way male authors had not really done before: as equals to men, and as the center of novels. They weren't pawns or objects to be won, but characters that, like Forster's men, were faced with constant scrutiny and moral quandaries. He also embraced the trappings of the modern novel, utilizing slang, vernacular, and colloquialisms.

# A BROKEN SYSTEM

Forster's novels told simple stories, which meant he could more easily allow the reader to understand his social commentary and symbolism without getting mired in plot points. His themes are most clear in 1908's *A Room with a View*, where Forster highlights the absurdity and "where does it end?" arbitrariness and superficiality of the British class system. In this novel, which contrasts the social freedoms of Italy with the stuffiness of England, the wealthy Lucy Honeychurch meets a man named George Emerson, who is not wealthy, when she's vacationing at an Italian hotel. They fall in love, but she rejects him because her cousin Charlotte doesn't approve of his family. She returns to England and becomes engaged to a proper, awful man. After running into George, she gets engaged to him instead, but gets disowned by her mother.

*Howards End* contained the same themes as *A Room with a View* and was a huge hit. It's about Margaret and Helen Schlegel (characters who represent the young, idealistic members of England's upper class) and Ruth Wilcox (meant to represent the conservative old guard), the owner of the house called Howards End. Henry Wilcox, Ruth's husband, and the Wilcox children are depicted as noticeably materialistic. Symbolically, Margaret marries Henry Wilcox after Ruth's death and brings this broken man back to Howards End, creating a link, if a fragile one, between the future and the past.

# IMPERIALISM

While visiting India in 1912 and serving in Egypt during World War I, Forster was exposed to the aggressive ways in which the English had attempted to civilize the world and impose its values on other cultures. Forster began to call out the dangers of imperialism and focused in on how the English exploited and fetishized the exotic for their own pleasure without seeing other humans as humans. These ideas come into play in *A Passage to India*.

In this title, Forster argues that the coexistence of the natural order and the onslaught of progress was tricky in India because it was a vast culture and land, and the English way of life was small and unimaginative. Imperialism overwhelmed India, and industrialism brought Dickensian nightmares to a new land. *Passage* ends with a symbolic impasse between Britain and India. Set during the Indian independence movement of the 1920s, this novel poses the question of whether or not an Indian and Englishman can actually be friends. *A Passage to India* was revolutionary, and the idea that it was controversial by design called out the idea that the English by and large didn't really see Indians as equals or even humans, let alone friends.

# TRUDGING FORWARD

The two World Wars made Forster reassess his values, and he embraced simpler ones in the face of modernity because he believed that modernity had only led to more efficient death and destruction. Reconciling humanity with nature and progress remained his ultimate ideal, but that ideal seemed impossible in the face of technology.

In World War II, he was recognized for his philosophy as much as his novels because he rejected all forms of totalitarianism (absolute and complete control by a central government), which to him included the expectations of being a "proper" English gentleman.

## Literary Lessons

Forster was uniquely qualified to speak about how proper and stifling the English could be and their propensity for repressing anything slightly out of the ordinary. Not only was he a gay man, but while serving with the Red Cross in Egypt during World War I he fell in love with an Egyptian bus driver. A same-sex relationship, not to mention an interracial one, was not something that would've been accepted at that time. He wrote the gay romance *Maurice* in 1912 that dealt with a similar theme, but it wasn't published until 1971, the year after Forster died.

In 1946, Cambridge gave Forster an honorary fellowship, and he became something of a literary and philosophical sage. Forster emphasized kindness and morality, which were unconnected to any ideology. But he's mainly remembered for his early novels, which came in the wake of romanticism and pinpointed and then amplified for the world the many problems of the ultimately doomed Victorian system.

# VIRGINIA WOOLF

A Movement of One's Own

Virginia Woolf (born Adeline Virginia Stephen) is heralded as one of the best modernist writers—if not the first and most influential of *modern* writers. Her life influenced her writing, and vice versa, as she dealt with deep depression and feminism in a time in which the world was not ready to explore those themes. Her background is as interesting as her work, which introduced complex and breathtaking new forms of storytelling (both in style and structure), as well as the incredibly personal, confessional, and unsettling parts of her own self she put on the page.

## EARLY LIFE

While Woolf would later use her position of prominence to agitate for more opportunities for women in writing, her early life was the perfect storm that allowed her to blossom as an artist. She was financially independent due to her wealthy parents, she was educated (albeit informally), and she wasn't dismissed by literary circles for having a talent that didn't befit her gender. Her father, Sir Leslie Stephen, was the editor for the sixty-two-volume *Dictionary of National Biography*, a compendium of the lives of important Britons. Her sister was a painter, and her brothers were prominent professors. But, despite being bright and trained to read and study by her father, she wasn't permitted to have a formal education. That was normal for the time, but she never forgot it, or forgave it—Woolf was ashamed for her entire life that she wasn't "properly" educated.

When their parents died, Virginia and her siblings moved from their Kensington estate to a rundown London neighborhood called Bloomsbury and held a *salon* (a gathering of intellectuals for the free exchange of ideas), later referred to as the Bloomsbury Group. Joining the Stephens were prominent London thinkers, including Leonard Woolf and John Maynard Keynes. The salon inspired Virginia to write, at first articles, book reviews, and literary criticism reviews for a number of London magazines before jumping into a novel called *The Voyage Out*. It took her five years to write, and it was a fairly standard novel. But it earned enough positive reviews to encourage her to write more, and to follow her instincts to stray outside the mainstream. And each piece of work she wrote played with form, structure, and language more than the one before it.

# A *LIGHT* AMONGST THE DARKNESS

In 1912, Virginia accepted a marriage proposal from Leonard Woolf, who proposed while Virginia was recovering from a mental breakdown in a pastoral nursing home. Woolf encouraged her writing, which he knew was better than his own. He was a novelist but founded Hogarth Press with Virginia, where they published obscure writers like T.S. Eliot, E.M. Forster ... and Virginia Woolf.

Hogarth published Virginia Woolf's *To the Lighthouse* in 1927, which unveiled her most innovative and important contributions to fiction: stories told in a nonlinear fashion, both in terms of events and the darting thoughts of the narrator. Today, this free-form prose style is called *stream of consciousness* for the way in which it realistically transcribes the inner workings of a brain lost in thought.

The literati of London praised her as one of the most staggeringly original writers in decades, but the lack of widespread acceptance exacerbated Woolf's depression. However, she stuck to her approach, and her works became even more experimental. She was a true modernist: The world itself was changing, and it was increasingly absurd. Artistic perception of that world had to change just as rapidly.

## Quotable Voices

"For now she need not think of anybody. She could be herself, by herself. And that was what now she often felt the need of—to think; well not even to think. To be silent; to be alone. All the being and the doing, expansive, glittering, vocal, evaporated; and one shrunk, with a sense of solemnity, to being oneself, a wedge-shaped core of darkness, something invisible to others . . . and this self having shed its attachments was free for the strangest adventures."

—To the Lighthouse

# MAKING *ROOM*

Virginia Woolf also became one of England's top literary critics and essayists. Her most influential work, *A Room of One's Own* (1929), was based on a series of feminist lectures she had delivered at Cambridge University. She laments the lack of working female writers in *A Room of One's Own*, but attributes that problem to specific social ills: that women can't be taken seriously as writers because they can't take themselves seriously as writers. Women were still seen as a lower social class and could rarely be financially independent to afford themselves the time to write. Nor were they educated, a symptom of both of those other symptoms.

Unlike other writers who merely just pointed out problems, Woolf called for an actual, pragmatic change to this problem: £500 per year as a stipend and private rooms set aside for female writers determined to have talent. The patronage program didn't quite take off, but it would serve as an inspiration for the artistic grant, which has given many writers the chance to just write.

Sadly, the depression so well expressed in Woolf's work would be her undoing. On March 28, 1941, she walked into the River Ouse with her pockets filled with stones and drowned. She was fifty-nine.

## Quotable Voices

"So long as you write what you wish to write, that is all that matters; and whether it matters for ages or only for hours, nobody can say."

—*A Room of One's Own*

# JAMES JOYCE

A Portrait of the Artist

Historically speaking, highbrow literature in the British Isles was not for or about the Irish. The Western literary tradition began with the epics of Homer and ancient Greek playwrights like Sophocles and Aeschylus, picked up with Anglo-Saxon poems like *Beowulf*, and continued on through to Chaucer, Shakespeare, Milton, and Dickens. By the twentieth century, there had been few major authors to come out of Ireland to write in the English language, which wasn't a surprise. By and large, Ireland resented England.

English was the language of the Church of England, which subjugated the island's preferred Catholicism, and English was the language spoken by foreign occupiers. English was the language of brutality to Ireland. But out of this problematic and complicated relationship between cultures and languages stepped James Joyce, who brought Ireland—and the culture of Dublin—into the highest realms of English literature.

## A MASTER OF LANGUAGES

Born in Dublin in 1882, James Joyce was the oldest of ten children. His father was a gifted singer who spent most of what little money the family had on drinking. Even as a child, James was keenly aware that he'd have to do as much as he possibly could himself to make his literary aspirations possible. For example, in order to fully understand the plays of Norwegian realist playwright Henrik Ibsen without the impediments of translators and their biases, Joyce taught himself

Norwegian. He majored in modern languages at University College Dublin, but after graduation moved to Paris to study to become a doctor. After his mother fell ill, Joyce briefly returned to Dublin and met and married his wife (and first reader), Nora Barnacle. Being a master of languages served him even then: They moved to Croatia, where Joyce taught English and learned Italian. He'd eventually be fluent in seventeen languages, from the standard European romance tongues (Italian, French) to Arabic, Sanskrit, Greek, and Norwegian, of course. All of them he learned so as to be able to read literature in its original form.

## Quotable Voices

"He asked himself what is a woman standing on the stairs in the shadow, listening to distant music, a symbol of. If he were a painter he would paint her in that attitude. Her blue felt hat would show off the bronze of her hair against the darkness and the dark panels of her skirt would show off the light ones. *Distant Music* he would call the picture if he were a painter."

—"The Dead"

# FOR DUBLIN

Joyce's first major work was the short-story collection *Dubliners*, published in 1914. A major work in realism (the literary attempt to present the human experience, including thoughts, feelings, and actions as true-to-life as possible), Joyce's collection was intended to depict "the significance of trivial things" and did so by showing ordinary people in their ordinary lives. He also wanted to show the world what life was really like in the underrepresented Irish capital of Dublin. The collection was also a strike for modernism. Thematically, it shows that life in Dublin was *not good*. The city that Joyce dubbed "the centre of paralysis of modern life" is crippled by the distant control of both the British Crown and the Catholic Church. The Dublin of Joyce's *Dubliners* is a living, breathing, dying thing—the final story in the collection is "The Dead."

## UP FROM THE ASHES

The follow-up to *Dubliners* was the stylistically different but thematically similar *A Portrait of the Artist as a Young Man* (1916). Initially intended to be a thinly veiled autobiography about his childhood, called *Stephen Hero*, Joyce hated the first draft so much that he threw it into a burning fire in his fireplace. Fortunately, Nora managed to fish it out, and Joyce reworked it into *Portrait*, which turned out to be much more experimental than a coming-of-age novel. It's written in an innovative stream-of-consciousness style—the thoughts hit the page as words and fragments, not necessarily clean narrative—which is used to depict internal life and thoughts as a reaction to the world. The way that those quick and stray thoughts are presented, while jumping back and forth with the same presentation of other thoughts, makes *Portrait* feel intimately inside of the narrator's brain. The story is more than a first-person narrative; it's *extremely* first person.

## A DAY IN THE LIFE

Joyce's following title was *Ulysses*. It's arguably one of the most ambitious and forward-thinking novels ever written, and it was about three leaps forward from the contemporary literature in Joyce's time.

It's so dense with obscure literary allusions, cultural references, jokes, puns, and references to contemporary Dublin that readers require phone-book-sized guidebooks to get the most out of it.

## Literary Lessons

Joyce and publisher Shakespeare and Company ran into legal trouble because *Ulysses*'s realism was too real. The chapter "Nausicaa" contains a scene of masturbation. The book was banned on obscenity charges until 1933. Many countries banned the book in its original form. The last to lift the ban? Ireland.

First serialized in the *Little Review* in the United States before being published in its entirety by Shakespeare and Company in France in 1922, *Ulysses* demonstrates one of Joyce's greatest innovations: How a story is told, that is, the language and syntax used, is inexorably wound up in the story itself. How a writer writes can determine what he or she can even write about. While this dark side of "write what you know" could limit some writers, it didn't hinder Joyce. His palette was so vast as to include a mastery of different forms and even language that he utilized whatever tool he wanted to tell each individual part of the story.

An example of this flexibility is that, in a section set in a maternity ward, Joyce starts writing in Old English verse before ending up in Irish vernacular—he gestates and "gives birth" to language. Another scene about fantasies and nightmares is written in a play script, because that's what Joyce deemed appropriate. All of this, served up stream-of-consciousness style in an extremely accurate imitation of thoughts flying through a mind, served to make readers intimately familiar with the characters' inner lives and thoughts, often to disorienting effect.

## Quotable Voices

"Every life is many days, day after day. We walk through ourselves, meeting robbers, ghosts, giants, old men, young men, wives, widows, brothers-in-love, but always meeting ourselves."

—*Ulysses*

Joyce needed multiple formats because *Ulysses* isn't one story. The book details as realistically as possible the goings-on of a (mostly fictionalized) single day in Dublin: June 16, 1904. *Ulysses* originated as a short story in *Dubliners* about a teacher who has an argument with a policeman, only to be rescued by a middle-aged Jewish man, an event Joyce witnessed in real life. But it just kept getting longer until Joyce decided he wanted to make a modern-day epic, like the Greeks did in ancient times. *Ulysses* is based on *The Odyssey*, and each of the book's eighteen episodes is a reworking or response to one of the eighteen sections of Homer's epic.

## Literary Lessons

Why did Joyce pick June 16, 1904, as *the* day to commit into history with *Ulysses*? Because that's the exact day he met Nora Barnacle, the woman who would be his wife.

The central character in *Ulysses* is Leopold Bloom, the middle-aged Irish Jewish man from the abandoned short story. The reader is immediately privy to Bloom's thought patterns as they veer all around, from needs to emotions, respectively, as he walks down the street. There are periods of frustration and boredom. Just like a regular day. And in spite of Joyce's new and innovative storytelling techniques, his work is often sentimental and sweet. In *Ulysses*, big events and important people were downplayed in favor of small happenings pictured through the eyes of regular folks.

## IN THE *WAKE* OF *ULYSSES*

How does an author follow a super experimental novel like *Ulysses* that breaks down form and rebuilds it back up into something both familiar and unfamiliar all at once? He deconstructs and builds up again, this time using the building blocks of language (including wordplay, jokes, and literary allusions). That's *Finnegan's Wake*, and it took Joyce seventeen years to write. With its invented words and stream of consciousness coming from the author himself (as opposed to the characters), it's about as easy to get through as reading *Beowulf* in Old English.

## LEGACY

Joyce suffered from eye problems throughout his life, and underwent a number of eye surgeries. Toward the end of his life he was nearly blind. He continued to write, using red crayon on giant sheets of paper so he could see his work.

Following an intestinal operation, Joyce died at the age of fifty-nine on January 13, 1941, at the Schwesternhaus von Rotenkreuz Hospital in Zurich, Switzerland. His legacy is celebrated on each June 16 with Bloomsday, a Dublin-wide city celebration, particularly in the real streets and bars mentioned by name in *Ulysses*.

# W.H. AUDEN

A New Classicist

Wystan Hugh Auden was born in York in 1907, the son of a father who was an early practitioner of the burgeoning science of psychology and a mother who was extremely religious. He was raised in a factory town, and he'd watch the mechanical machinery run whenever he could, but he also served as a choir boy in the local church. Religious services also gave him a sensitivity to language, which would pay off with entry into Oxford. In his writing, Auden would seek to reconcile those two concepts prominent in his childhood:

- science
- religion

His dueling interests continued to compete for attention as Auden grew up. He studied both science and English literature, which he didn't care for, because the curriculum focused too heavily on the romantics and their emotional style. Fortunately for him, he came of age in the early twentieth century, when experimentation and a simplification of poetic forms was all the rage. Auden's contribution? He was the first English poet to use the imagery and terminology of psychology. Auden coupled that with an interest and use of Anglo-Saxon language and themes that made his work difficult to understand at times, and provided it with an air of mysticism.

Auden is one of the last "household name" poets (along with Dylan Thomas, T.S. Eliot, and Philip Larkin). His works are highly brainy, scientific even, and run counter to the feelings-based poetry that dominated the history of English poetry. Auden wrote of science and reason, not the unreliability of emotion.

## Quotable Voices

> "Such was this doctor: still at eighty he wished
> to think of our life from whose unruliness
> so many plausible young futures
> with threats or flattery ask obedience,
> but his wish was denied him: he closed his eyes
> upon that last picture, common to us all,
> of problems like relatives gathered
> puzzled and jealous about our dying."

—"In Memory of Sigmund Freud"

# TO AMERICA

In January 1939, Auden fled World War II and settled in the United States. That same year he met his lifelong companion, Chester Kallman ,and, in 1946, he became a U.S. citizen. Abandoning his brain-based poetry, later in his career his work became almost entirely religious in nature; he even rewrote much of his earlier work to bring it in line with his new philosophies, trading in his left-wing politics for a moderate-to-conservative stance as well as a recommitment to Christianity.

The poetry world rolled with the changes, however—writing about new topics spoke to his versatility. He returned to Oxford to be a professor in the 1950s, shortly after winning the 1948 Pulitzer Prize for his collection *The Age of Anxiety*. Auden died of heart failure at age 66 in 1973.

# DYLAN THOMAS

The Clear Expression of Mixed Feelings

Dylan Thomas was a larger-than-life character, a boisterous Welsh poet whose one line about death and perseverance is among the most memorable and insightful poetic passages of the twentieth century: "rage, rage against the dying of the light." He wrote from the heart, and was a passionate poet with more in common with the old romantic style during an era in which poetry had taken a brainy, rational direction (exemplified by W.H. Auden and T.S. Eliot). Thomas is a national hero in Wales, although he never learned the local language, opting instead to be a master of the English poem with his emotionally resonant, electric, and urgent style.

While Thomas's poems are emotionally driven and lyrical and can come across as flippant or off-the-cuff, he tirelessly edited and rewrote until he got to what he thought was perfection. He reportedly would make up to 500 revisions of one poem. Each time he'd write it out over again to better feel the words taking shape, and to see if he was on the right track. It was brutal labor, and it's probably why Thomas called poetry "that sullen art."

But while Thomas's process was intellectual and precise, you can't say the same about his poetry, especially when Thomas is compared to, say, T.S. Eliot or W.H. Auden. He didn't much write about the nature of art or social problems. Instead, he focused on intense emotion and organically transitioning imagery. In a letter to a friend, Thomas described his approach:

"I make one image—though 'make' is not the right word; I let, perhaps, an image be 'made' emotionally in me and then apply to it what intellectual and critical forces I possess—let it breed another, let that image contradict the first."

By his own reasoning, Thomas was more in line with the romantic poets than the modernists.

## THE CELEBRITY

The relatable, gut feelings that Thomas put on the page made him a very popular poet in his lifetime, and his collections were among the bestselling in the mid-twentieth century. Critics, however, didn't much care for him. He was widely accused of burying meaning in his poetry on purpose; critics of the time were just more used to the intellectualism and hopelessness of the modernist poets. Thomas wrote from the heart, which can be complicated and contradictory, as he openly acknowledged.

Thomas is among a handful of British poets well known, at least by name, in the United States. Like Mark Twain or Charles Dickens, he had a big personality, and it served him well on extensive lecture and reading tours in the Americas. The tours were a hit—Thomas struck quite an image. He showed up for readings shabbily dressed, willing to have a drink or two with his fans, and delivered his performance-ready poetry in a thick, working-class accent.

Thomas is also among the first writers to utilize electronic media. He was a popular presence on English radio, reading his poems and presenting radio plays. His single most famous dramatic piece is the radio drama *Under Milk Wood*. Produced posthumously by the BBC in 1954, it's set in the Welsh seaside town of Llareggub. Presented in alliterative prose, it's a melancholy work about a dressmaker, her lover, and a bunch of townies who talk about their dreams and their boring daily lives. The play was first performed on stage in New York City at the 92nd Street Y in May 1953, with Thomas reading two of the parts himself. A few months later, in November, he died in New York after a night of drinking. His last words were reportedly:

"I've had eighteen straight whiskies. I think that's the record. After thirty-nine years this is all I've done."

Even after his death, Thomas remained a major favorite of the poets in the New Apocalypse movement, a 1940s and beyond romantic, passionately driven reaction against the perceived dry and emotionally distant poetry of other poets of the era.

## Quotable Voices

"Time passes. Listen. Time passes.
Come closer now.
Only you can hear the houses sleeping in the streets in the slow deep salt and silent black, bandaged night."

—from *Under Milk Wood*

# Chapter 7

# Contemporary English Literature

Twentieth-century English literature (and beyond) can be characterized by rapid expansion on two fronts. On one end was the modernist movement, where writers experimented with the very building blocks of written communication. At the other end, literature took hold as a form of entertainment. In addition, the standards of narrative writing developed by writers in England became the standards for storytelling around the world as other English-speaking countries continued to develop their own literary identities. These standards also influenced the ways stories were told in emerging media worldwide, such as film, radio, new forms of theater, and television.

The second half of the twentieth century allowed room in English literature for more voices and styles. Imperialism, colonialism, and war had spread the English language around the world. More English readers were created, which led to more English writers. In that regard, English literature became the world's literature, and England itself became a more ethnically diverse place.

English literature kept pace with that change, while it also did what it had always done: address what "Englishness" meant, even as that was an evolving and growing notion. Major literary works of the late twentieth and early twenty-first centuries added to the literary canon while also being greatly influenced by and commenting on their predecessors. For example, J.K. Rowling wrote fantasy fiction in a genre created by earlier stalwarts J.R.R. Tolkien and C.S. Lewis; Harold Pinter's plays directly descend from the stinging cultural send-ups written by George Bernard Shaw decades earlier.

But no matter if it's a new take on an old form or a revival of an old style, contemporary literature in England isn't all that different from what it was in the time of Shakespeare, Chaucer, or even *Beowulf*: Yes, it's about England, and Western civilization, but it's really about conveying the human experience as honestly, realistically, and artistically as possible.

# SIR ARTHUR CONAN DOYLE

It's Elementary

Sir Arthur Conan Doyle's Sherlock Holmes joins the pantheon of iconic British characters, along with King Arthur and Robin Hood, as one of the great literary heroes, but he was also a perplexing modern character: He's inscrutable, almost impenetrable, and so intelligent as to be a figure of awe. He's also a jumble of contradictions. Sherlock is brilliant at his job, but he's socially maladjusted. He's the greatest detective in the world who notices details with an almost supernatural ability, but he's also addicted to drugs. He's a passionate truth-seeker, but struggles with other emotions. Sherlock is a complex character, to say the least, but his contradictions provide depth, and make him seem all the more real. And he's just one part of an all-time great literary duo along with his partner in crime fighting, Dr. John Watson, the audience surrogate and point of view from which the Sherlock stories are told.

Doyle's writing style is clearly Victorian, but he was also a forward thinker. Like other holdovers from the Victorian era, the prose is florid and uses too many words, except when Sherlock is talking. Sherlock doesn't mince words. He's terse and blunt, while the other characters speak like Victorians. Sherlock also uses logic to dispel the myth and ghost worlds of the Victorian era. In his mind rational thought always prevails over hearsay and hogwash. So while the Holmes stories are highly utilitarian and populist, they're modernist all the same; it's modernism for the people.

# THE GAME IS AFOOT

Doyle studied medicine, just like Watson, but in 1880s London, a man could make more money writing for the many popular periodicals than he could working as an eye doctor. After writing various stories and earning a tidy living at it, Doyle struck on the Holmes formula in 1887 with *A Study in Scarlet*. It introduced the characters of Holmes and Watson, fully developed. Holmes is an ultra-intelligent, drug-addicted, violin-playing police consultant who uses minute observation and logical deduction to solve a murder mystery. (Doyle actually based Holmes on a doctor he'd studied with named Joseph Bell who was also an extremely good observer of details.) *A Study in Scarlet* was published for a Christmas magazine, and it didn't garner much attention. Nor did Doyle's next Holmes novel, *The Sign of the Four*, which added to the mix the Baker Street Irregulars, the street hooligans who act as informants and errand boys for Holmes and Watson.

## Literary Lessons

Sherlock technically doesn't use deduction to solve mysteries. Deduction eliminates possibilities until the correct theory remains. What Sherlock uses is *abductive reasoning*, which involves careful consideration of evidence, observation, and outside data that is used to create a stab at a theory.

Holmes only became a phenomenon when Doyle made the stories more accessible by writing them as short stories instead of novels. When they were published in the *Strand Magazine* in 1891, Holmes became a smash. When two years' worth of standalone stories were published as *The Adventures of Sherlock Holmes* in 1892, it was a bestseller.

# A BRIEF AND UNFORTUNATE DEATH

And yet even though he'd cynically conceived the stories as a money-making scheme, Doyle had already tired of writing stories for the character by the time that first collection was released. He was an artist, itching to try something new. In 1891, Doyle published his passion project, an epic novel about the Hundred Years' War called *The White Company*. Doyle believed (or hoped) that this would be the singular achievement among a larger body of work for which he would be remembered, his own *War and Peace*, *Middlemarch*, or *A Tale of Two Cities*. It was critically acclaimed, but didn't sell particularly well: Regular readers wanted more Sherlock Holmes. Whether out of spite or the desire to write a novel, in the 1893 collection *The Memoirs of Sherlock Holmes*, Doyle wrote a new story called "The Final Problem." Sherlock dies at the end.

Doyle got his wish, and spent six years writing other things that sold well because they were written by the creator of Sherlock Holmes, but nothing as iconic as Sherlock Holmes, and certainly nothing that's read much today. *The Exploits of Brigadier Gerard*, anyone? How about *Sir Nigel*, a prequel to *The White Company*, which Doyle personally thought was superior?

## Literary Lessons

In none of Sir Arthur Conan Doyle's Sherlock Holmes novels or stories did Sherlock actually utter the catchphrase most associated with the character, "Elementary, Watson!" Four times, however, he said, "Exactly, my dear Watson!"

Ultimately Doyle gave in to the public and revived Sherlock, the character and the stories, in 1899. Reserving himself the right to walk away whenever he wanted, Doyle first claimed that any new Sherlock stories he wrote took place *before* Sherlock died, but he quickly abandoned that conceit and churned out more stories than he ever had. The stories resumed appearing in the *Strand*, including what's arguably the most well-known tale, the supernatural-leaning *The Hound of the Baskervilles* (1902). When it was all said and done, Doyle wrote fifty-six Sherlock stories and four Sherlock novels. Amazingly, all of them are still in print.

## A KNIGHT'S TALE

Doyle's most famous non-Sherlock work is undoubtedly an exhaustive, journalistic account of the Boer War (albeit one heavily biased and congratulatory toward England) called *The Great Boer War*. For that book (and also for Sherlock), Doyle was knighted in 1902. One other notable book in Doyle's oeuvre was *The Lost World*. Like the Sherlock books, it was rip-roaring commercial fiction for the masses. Set amidst the world of European colonialism in Africa, an explorer heads deep into the continent and finds a prehistoric civilization—including dinosaurs. Like Sherlock, the main character, George Edward Challenger, is quite memorable—but he's flamboyant, arrogant, and fearless.

Mysteries and crime fiction still draw on the formulas set forth by Doyle, who gave birth to the detective story. The Sherlock stories were also a landmark in popular fiction and narrative. One of the most popular and enduring characters ever, more than 100 years later, Sherlock's influence on psychology and crime-solving remain. Sherlock is still a major pop culture presence, too, with a film series, a British TV series, and an American TV series all in production in the 2010s.

# GEORGE BERNARD SHAW

Ireland's Shakespeare

George Bernard Shaw's work was a pragmatic response to the defeatism of modernism. Much of modernism was about the individual writer coming to terms with a society that was hopelessly broken, and that there was nothing the individual personally could do to remedy social ills or even man's nasty nature. The medium fit the message: Novels and poems in this regard were personal, introspective, and interior. George Bernard Shaw's medium also fit his message: He wasn't wrapped up in his own thoughts and interior life. He wrote social commentary—mostly plays—performed so that crowds could hear his very external message of calling out society's ills and his suggestions on how to actually fix those problems.

Shaw ranks as the most dominant and lasting English playwright of the early twentieth century. (He'd have that achievement in volume alone: He wrote more than sixty plays.) His style was so seeped in social commentary, irony, and caustic wit that any writer who's done anything similar is labeled "Shavian."

## HIGHLY THEATRICAL

George Bernard Shaw was born in Dublin in 1856 to parents who owned a lot of land but didn't have a lot of money. His father was a failed corn merchant and alcoholic, so his mother gave piano lessons to support the family. Shaw hated his schools (he compared them to prisons), preferring to educate himself the way he wanted to be educated, which for him meant devouring the romantic poets and going to the theater as often as he could. As a young man he moved to London to see as many plays as possible and to attend lectures at the British Museum. That relocation put him on the path to a career as a writer, composing satirical lectures: social commentaries mocking the repression of Victorian England with its many rules regarding marriage, education, politics, and religion. He wrote dozens of political essays and books in his lifetime advocating revolutionary principles such as:

- socialism
- Stalinism
- women's rights
- vegetarianism

Shaw was also something of a crank: He was an outspoken critic of a lot of Victorian literature on the grounds that it encouraged "bad behavior," particularly the rule-breaking misfits of Charles Dickens's novels.

## Quotable Voices

"The English have no respect for their language, and will not teach their children to speak it. . . . It is impossible for an Englishman to open his mouth without making some other Englishman hate or despise him. . . . The reformer England needs today is an energetic phonetic enthusiast: that is why I have made such a one the hero of a popular play."

—from the preface to *Pygmalion*

By 1895, Shaw was the *Saturday Review*'s theater critic, but he was also writing plays himself. He admired the Norwegian playwright Henrik Ibsen, whose plays discussed social problems such as sexism and repression. Shaw wanted to do the same thing, in English, for English society. His plays are one part social commentary, one part satire. Still, Shaw's dramas are highly realistic, delivered in real and direct speech, with his characters often clearly stating the author's point.

## GETTING SERIOUS

Many of Shaw's plays have not aged well, because they are less about the structure and wordplay than they are about delivering a very clear message about a social issue. This would come to define twentieth-century theater—plays are generally "serious" and musicals are "light." Ironically, Shaw's most famous play, *Pygmalion*, calls attention to class differences between a Cockney flower girl and a haughty professor who teaches the girl to speak proper English. It was turned into the musical *My Fair Lady*, which differs from its source material in that it ends in true love for the flower girl and professor. Shaw's original intent was actually to call attention to the spread of lazy English grammar.

Shaw was so forward minded and socially oriented in his plays that he rejected the artistic artifice of the form. He even hated Shakespeare. In 1949, he wrote *Shakes versus Shav*, a Punch and Judy puppet show where he fights with Shakespeare over "bardolatry" (an excessive worshipping of William Shakespeare) and who is the greatest writer. Guess who wins?

Shortly after writing his puppet show, Shaw died at the age of ninety-four. His work lives on, both on the stage and in the world at large. Many of his plays, especially *Pygmalion, Major Barbara,* and *Saint Joan,* are still widely produced. And his social views, such as feminism and vegetarianism, have gained far wider acceptance in the last century.

## Literary Lessons

In 1925, Shaw was awarded the Nobel Prize for Literature for his body of work. But he declined the prize money—about 118,000 Swedish kronor, the equivalent of $450,000 in today's dollars—because he said he didn't need it. Instead, the money was used to set up a cultural relations board between Sweden and the UK.

# JOSEPH CONRAD

Into Darkness

Joseph Conrad brought a very new voice to the literature of England. Raised by Polish parents in Russia, he was primarily a sailor and explorer who traveled far and wide, and who represented a dark side of the fun adventures undertaken by Robert Louis Stevenson or Daniel Defoe. By the time Conrad became an English citizen in his forties, he had faced down—and written about—the dark and mysterious side of English colonialism and the devastation that it had wrought on both the world and the human psyche.

## EXILED

Józef Konrad Korzeniowski was born in 1857 in a region of Russia that's now the Ukraine. His parents were members of the *szlachta* class, or Polish nobles, living under tsarist Russian rule. His father, Apollo Korzeniowski, translated great authors like Victor Hugo and Shakespeare into Polish, and he was also a nationalist, in favor of both freeing the serfs and Polish independence. As a result, the family was under surveillance, and in 1861, both of Korzeniowski's parents were arrested for being part of a Polish anti-Russian conspiracy. They were sent to live in exile in the remote, cold, and barren Vologda province in northern Russia. By 1869, when Korzeniowski was twelve, both his parents had contracted tuberculosis and died.

He was raised by an uncle in Poland and was in and out of schools until he ran away to Marseilles, France, at sixteen and joined the merchant marines. He went to France because his governess had taught him French; he went into the merchant marines because he wanted to visit "the dark continent" of Africa. (It also helped him avoid being drafted into the Russian army.)

## LIFE AT SEA

After five years with French crews in the merchant marines, he tried to commit suicide to escape huge gambling debts. His uncle paid off his debts, but Korzeniowski was kicked out of the French service. He then joined an English crew, whereupon he changed his name to Joseph Conrad (and became a citizen of England in 1888). Through his adventures, he sailed to South America, the Caribbean, India, Australia, and finally, after nearly seventeen years of traveling, Africa in 1890.

The trip rattled him, both emotionally and physically. Forced to take command of a steamboat for the first time, Conrad had to pick up and transport a Belgian trader named Georges Antoine Klein. Along the way, Klein died and Conrad contracted malaria. With that medical problem making his gout and depression even worse, Conrad decided to leave the life of adventure behind and settle permanently in England. Aside from writing in his journals, Conrad didn't think about becoming a writer until he was nearly forty. In 1896, he married the daughter of a publisher, which led to friendships with major literary figures such as H.G. Wells and Ford Madox Ford, the writer and editor who had discovered T.S. Eliot. Encouraged to parlay his real-life adventures into adventure fiction, Conrad wrote the fun and boisterous *Almayer's Folly*, a romp set in Borneo.

# OH, THE HORRORS

Once Conrad started writing, he got real serious, real quick. He continued to write about sailors and explorers, except in his new stories they were European explorers being brutal to others and receiving brutality thousands of miles from home in untamed, "savage" lands. In a callback to the darker impulses of romanticism, Conrad wrote about the power of the individual as well as nature, only he wrote about nature's brutality and indifference, not its beauty. Conrad's novels were a major influence on modernism, primarily for the stark psychological realism and Conrad's exposure of the naturally dark side of human nature.

## Quotable Voices

"It's extraordinary how we go through life with eyes half shut, with dull ears, with dormant thoughts. Perhaps it's just as well; and it may be that it is this very dullness that makes life to the incalculable majority so supportable and so welcome. Nevertheless, there can be but few of us who had never known one of these rare moments of awakening when we see, hear, understand ever so much—everything—in a flash—before we fall back again into our agreeable somnolence."

—Lord Jim

His novel *Lord Jim* concerns a cowardly sailor, Jim (no last name is given), who flees to a remote South Seas island to avoid the fallout over his cowardly act of abandoning the passengers on a sinking boat that he crewed on. On the island, Jim comes into power and comes to terms, fatally, with his past action.

Conrad's next book was his masterpiece, *Heart of Darkness*. It's a slow-moving, psychologically dense and foreboding novella about a British man's journey deep into the Congo to locate the mysterious (and probably evil) Kurtz, a former trader who became the self-appointed lord of the land.

## Quotable Voices

"It seems to me I am trying to tell you a dream—making a vain attempt, because no relation of a dream can convey the dream-sensation, that commingling of absurdity, surprise, and bewilderment in a tremor of struggling revolt, that notion of being captured by the incredible which is of the very essence of dreams . . . No, it is impossible; it is impossible to convey the life-sensation of any given epoch of one's existence—that which makes its truth, its meaning—its subtle and penetrating essence. It is impossible. We live, as we dream—alone."

—*Heart of Darkness*

*Lord Jim* and *Heart of Darkness* are companion pieces: Haunting, vivid, and even lurid imagery is used throughout both to contemplate the good and evil parts of human nature (mostly the evil part)—and how those labels are arbitrary, ambiguous, and constantly blurred. To explore a variety of moral issues and man's leaning toward corruption and self-delusion, Conrad employs an *anti-hero,* a protagonist or hero who isn't typically heroic—they're dishonest, bitter, or selfish instead of kind, brave, or idealistic. Of course, those internal struggles parallel the big political stories of the time period: One man's journey into the Congo in *Heart of Darkness* and the horrors he sees are a very clear comment on colonialism and Europe's ill-conceived drive to conquer Africa.

# THE WORLD COMES TO ENGLAND

Conrad's concepts about stark psychological realism and the dark side of human nature would influence the modernists and their commitment to provide as realistic a depiction of human thought as possible. These concepts also influenced the *existentialists* (a group of twentieth-century philosophers who believed that life was meaningless beyond any meaning that humans arbitrarily provide) like Albert Camus, whose *The Stranger* shares *Heart of Darkness*'s blunt, matter-of-fact, and mundane descriptions of evil. Southern gothic American writers such as Flannery O'Connor and William Faulkner were also influenced by Conrad.

## Literary Lessons

For his many contributions to English literature, Conrad was offered a knighthood in May 1924 from Prime Minister Ramsay MacDonald. But Conrad turned it down, just like he'd turned down five honorary degrees. Conrad died in August 1924, but he's been far outlived by his work. *Heart of Darkness* is one of the most commonly taught books in American high school and college literature classes. It also served as the basis for Francis Ford Coppola's harrowing 1979 war movie, *Apocalypse Now*.

Conrad represents the first of the "outsiders" in English fiction. English by choice and not by birth, and spending the first four decades of his life everywhere but England, he was a citizen of the world and an astute observer and student of humans at their darkest moments. Conrad's success foretold a revolution of multicultural voices that would embody and expand English literature in the twentieth and twenty-first centuries. English literature wasn't just written about England for the English anymore, and it would never be again.

# WILLIAM GOLDING

*Lord of the Flies*

One theme of modernism that gained steam after World War I was an attempt to make sense of the death and destruction, an acceptance of humanity's innate darkness. After World War II, this theme was revived when authors wondered if humankind would ever truly be able to put aside its savage and brutal nature—its dark side, really. In a biblical sense, this is original sin; in a modern sense, it's man's inescapable brutality. The prime example of this philosophy in action is William Golding's 1954 novel, *Lord of the Flies*.

## TRY, TRY AGAIN

William Golding was raised in Cornwall and educated at Oxford. And following the commercial failure of his first book, *Poems*, Golding took a job teaching English at Bishop Wordsworth's School in Salisbury in 1935. He continued teaching after a stint in the Royal Navy in World War II, but he never gave up his dream of being a writer—he would work on his projects during class, and would assign his students tasks like counting up the words on his submissions before sending them to publishers. And there were *a lot* of publishers. In the early 1950s, Golding sent his manuscript for *Lord of the Flies* to twenty-one different publishers. They all rejected it, until a rookie editor at Faber and Faber spotted it in a trash can and fished it out. Another editor had written on it, "absurd & uninteresting."

# ISLAND OF MISFIT BOYS

In *Lord of the Flies*, during a nuclear war in the not-very-distant future, a group of British schoolboys (like the ones Golding taught in Salisbury) are evacuated. Their plane crashes into the ocean and they take refuge on an island. The events of the plot serve highly symbolic functions: The island represents society, and the characters different types of people. Brave Ralph, for example, is the noble if naive leader; his advisor Piggy is rational and intellectual; Jack also wants to lead and lures everyone away from Ralph and Piggy's reasonable methods to savage, selfish survivalism, invoking fear of an unseen "beast" that's a threat to them all. They're ultimately rescued and pretend that nothing happened, choosing to keep their darkest secrets stifled just below the surface—as it's human nature to combat human nature. Golding was certainly using *Lord of the Flies* to comment on World War II and the rebuilding of Europe afterward.

*Lord of the Flies* is an unrelentingly hopeless and pessimistic novel. Golding's psychologically realistic (and brutal) characterizations were pulled from observations of his own students, as well as his own memories as a childhood bully and his time in the navy. Golding later said:

> "I began to see what people were capable of doing . . . Anyone who moved through those years without understanding that man produces evil as a bee produces honey, must have been blind or wrong in the head."

In both the modernist and even existentialist tradition, Golding suggests, with both the boys on the island and in the wake of World War II, that humans are not just dark-sided but by their very nature savage, primal, barbaric, and evil. It is natural to degenerate into fear, violence, and savagery to rule and survive. These themes and more are very easy to understand because Golding loads *Lord of the Flies* with very clear symbols. In addition to big ones like the island equaling the world and the boys being society, for example, Piggy's glasses, a tool that makes objects appear clearer, represent reason and civility—and it's certainly meaningful when those glasses get crushed.

## Literary Lessons

Not only were publishers uninterested at first in *Lord of the Flies,* readers were as well. In the first year after it was released by Faber and Faber, the novel sold just more than 4,000 copies and went out of print. But it remained a popular title among literature teachers in the UK and the U.S. Word of mouth saved it from obscurity and by 1962, it was back in print, and became assigned reading in hundreds of classrooms.

Golding's boldest move is using children as his mirror for society. Not yet clouded by society or the burdens of adulthood, they are, Golding suggests, pure, and pure in their humanity. And yet they still fall prey to their darkest and most savage impulses. Ironically, *Lord of the Flies* is most often read today in junior highs and high schools around the world—when most readers pick up the novel for the first time, they're the same age as the characters.

# AN UNCOMFORTABLE REALITY

*Lord of the Flies* is and isn't a modernist novel. It is modernist in that it ends ambiguously with no moral lesson being imparted, and only bad feelings conjured up. It isn't a modernist novel in that Golding tells his story in a simple, straightforward manner with lots of allegory and doesn't play with form and function and syntax the way James Joyce or Virginia Woolf did. Golding structures it like a fable, in which characters aren't quite well rounded, flawed, or realistic— they embody one particular theme or value. (Jack is savagery; Piggy is reason; etc.) The characters do have some ambiguity, however; if they were drawn entirely as one-note characters, the book would be overly moralistic and far less visceral than it is. Inner conflicts are placed in the characters to heighten the problems with the real-world values they represent. Piggy is the scientist, and is rational and smarter than the other boys, but he is absolutely powerless in keeping them in line.

*Lord of the Flies* is by far Golding's most enduring work, although he did write bestselling, prize-winning novels on similar themes of man's inhumanity, such as *Rites of Passage*, *The Pyramid*, and *Pincher Martin*. It's a body of work that won the former schoolteacher the 1983 Nobel Prize for Literature.

# J.R.R. TOLKIEN AND C.S. LEWIS

Two Towers

J.R.R. Tolkien and C.S. Lewis were close friends, and they had a lot in common. Both were Oxford professors in the mid-twentieth century, and both were very religious—Tolkien, in fact, helped Lewis convert to Christianity, even though Lewis joined the Church of England instead of Tolkien's Catholic Church. And, of course, both wrote tremendously popular and influential multivolume works of fantasy (or *speculative fiction*) to explain their point of view and academic interests, and to make sense of an increasingly complicated and confusing world.

## TOLKIEN

John Ronald Reuel Tolkien was born to English parents in South Africa in 1892. His childhood was tough and tragic. His father died when he was a baby, and his Protestant father's family financially cut off Tolkien, his mother, and his brother when they converted to Catholicism. Then Tolkien's mother died, and the Tolkien boys were placed under the care of a parish priest. Nevertheless, Tolkien had an incredible gift for language, not just English but the science of linguistics. He could easily learn, speak, and read new languages, and could quickly grasp their structures and construction. Tolkien rode this ability to an Oxford education, where he remained throughout his adulthood as a professor of both literature and languages.

Tolkien primarily wrote what the academic life required him to: scores of critical studies and analyses. He could read Old English to such an extent that he produced one of the first modern-day assessments of *Beowulf*. "*Beowulf*: The Monsters and the Critics" was first given as a speech then subsequently published in the journal *Proceedings of the British Academy* in 1936, and it single-handedly is credited with igniting interest in the study of the ancient epic poem as part of the British literary heritage.

*Beowulf* was a favorite text of Tolkien, and it inspired him to write his own fiction. Tolkien wanted to write extremely old-fashioned epics like *Beowulf* so as to provide England its own similar mythology, or at least in addition to the King Arthur and Robin Hood tales. But myths to Tolkien were more than just made-up stories. To him, myths expressed transcendent, undeniable truths about life *through* made-up stories. The extremely religious Tolkien held that to read or write mythology was almost a form of prayer, a way to meditate on life's great truths and connect to the universe. Tolkien wrote:

> "We have come from God, and only through myth, through storytelling, can we aspire to the life we were made for with God."

The mechanics of the Anglo-Saxon language of *Beowulf* also inspired Tolkien's creative work. His scholarly understanding of language made him a gifted mimic, enabling him to create out of whole cloth new languages (including syntax and grammar) that *sound* real, interwoven with his invented mythology that also felt like it could've been real. That's how Tolkien created the vast universe of Middle-earth, the setting for the hero's quest children's book *The Hobbit* (1937) and its sequel, *The Lord of the Rings* (1954–1955), an increasingly dark trilogy in which good triumphs over evil . . . but just barely. The latter is allegorical to the events in Europe over the course of World War II.

In *The Hobbit*, a wizard named Gandalf recruits a hobbit named Bilbo Baggins, a gentle, half-sized homebody to help a group of dwarves reclaim their ancestral home and their gold from an evil dragon. Along the way, Bilbo finds a magical ring, which then drives the plot of *The Lord of the Rings*. The ring brings special powers to whoever wears it, despite its life-sucking evil powers. Armies amass to get the ring, and Bilbo's nephew, Frodo Baggins, must take a journey to destroy the ring in the fires of Mount Doom.

## Quotable Voices

> "But in the end it's only a passing thing,
> this shadow; even darkness must pass."
>
> —*The Lord of the Rings*

The phenomenal, enduring success of Tolkien's epic gives a lot of credence to this theory that reading mythology, along with religion, is a way for humans to fulfill the deep need to tap into something larger than themselves. Its influence on fantasy fiction—all fantasy fiction owes a debt to Tolkien—suggests the same. Epic tales are most enjoyable and most profound if they are told as part of a grand, multibook "universe" of characters, imagined histories, and languages. *The Lord of the Rings*, the Harry Potter series, and George R.R. Martin's *A Song of Ice and Fire* novels are just a few examples of this; all are multibook series with completely realized worlds and richly imagined characters and mythologies, and they have large and devoted fan bases.

Despite Tolkien's foundation in linguistics and mythological studies (and pedigree as an Oxford professor), his novels were not taken seriously as literature until more than a decade after they were initially published. They sold only modestly, and Middle-earth was on its way to oblivion when it was embraced by 1960s counterculture types. These "hippies" strongly identified with hobbits—simple, friendly people trying to live simple lives of happiness and creature comforts and wanting nothing to do with the great evils threatening the world. The rest is history and *The Hobbit* and *The Lord of the Rings* are now among the bestselling books ever published in English.

# LEWIS

Clive Staples Lewis was born in Belfast in 1898, although when he was a toddler he decided his name was Jack, and that's what friends and family called him for the rest of his life. As a child, he already had the beginnings of his future fantasy work. Lewis and his brother created an intricate fantasy world called Boxen, where they'd play every day, interacting with imaginary talking beasts and gallant kings and warriors. After a stint in World War I ended prematurely when he was struck with shrapnel, Lewis graduated from Oxford with degrees in literature and philosophy and stayed at the university to teach. He joined an informal literary group of professors called the Inklings, which is where he met Tolkien, and was moved to convert to Christianity in 1931.

While Tolkien was a practicing Christian, he wrote more about universal spiritual themes. Lewis, however, wrote fiction and nonfiction specifically within the realm of Christianity. He was both an intellectual and an apologist, his literary response to what he thought was the godlessness of modernism. Lewis didn't outright preach his faith, choosing instead to argue in favor of its tenets with logic and other techniques, including emotional appeals. In doing so, he became one of the most influential (and bestselling) philosophers in recent history.

Lewis's first major work of fiction was *Out of the Silent Planet* (1938). Ostensibly about a group of humans who leave Earth to settle on Malacandra and live among its residents, it's an allegorical tale about racism and colonialism. When England became involved in World War II, Lewis served by writing and delivering radio sermons. In addition to providing comfort to a war-torn nation, it marked the beginning of Lewis's Christian *apologetic* works—using narrative fiction to demystify and explain Christianity.

## Quotable Voices

"Indeed the safest road to Hell is the gradual one—
the gentle slope, soft underfoot, without sudden turnings,
without milestones, without signposts."

—*The Screwtape Letters*

One of Lewis's major works in that genre is *The Screwtape Letters*. It's an *epistolary novel*, meaning the story is told through a series of letters. In the book, the correspondence is between a high-ranking demon named Screwtape and his idiotic nephew named Wormwood. The letters concern a human Christian convert (referred to as "The Patient") and the attempts to lure him to the dark side. Screwtape and Wormwood are ultimately unsuccessful. Lewis wrote it as a witty cautionary tale to suggest that souls are constantly in flux, and that while goodness and darkness are parts of being human, it's a conscious choice to decide which side to follow. In using demons as characters, it's a throwback to Milton's *Paradise Lost*, and the discussion of men's capacity for evil is right in line with other twentieth-century works, particularly *Lord of the Flies*. Unlike many of his colleagues, however, Lewis is of the mind that good will always triumph over evil.

While *The Screwtape Letters* and other apologetic works like *Mere Christianity* are explicitly and directly about Christianity, The Chronicles of Narnia novels are allegorical fiction. This series contains seven books that tell a story for children through symbolism and adventure of a world inhabited by talking animals, particularly Aslan the lion, a clear Christ figure.

# GEORGE ORWELL

Big Brother Is Watching

George Orwell is the pen name of Eric Blair, an essayist, novelist, critic, and social agitator. Born in India in 1903 when it was a British territory, Blair returned to England as a baby with his family and attended St. Cyprian's School, a private school, on scholarship. There he learned of the social divisions still holding firm in England in the 1920s, a generation removed from the Victorian era. His fellow students rejected him because he was merely middle class, while all the other boys were wealthy. Unable to afford college, he joined the Indian Imperial Police and served in Burma. There he saw firsthand the effects of British colonialism and poor treatment of locals, which made Blair want to be a champion of the oppressed.

## Quotable Voices

"Not to expose your true feelings to an adult seems to be instinctive from the age of seven or eight onwards."

—"Such, Such Were the Joys"

# GETTING EXPERIMENTAL

Blair returned to England and as a social experiment made himself "classless." In other words, he voluntarily lived in both London and Paris as if he were extremely poor so as to better empathize with those who actually were. While well intentioned (he wouldn't wear a coat in the winter to see what it felt like to be cold, for example) but somewhat misguided (he also refused to use table manners, because that's what he thought poor people did), he got ill quite a few times and abandoned the experiment when he began to slip into actual poverty. But it all informed his work: In 1933, he turned his experiences into the memoir-with-an-angle *Down and Out in Paris*, published under the name George Orwell (inspired by the River Orwell in Suffolk). A hip, new voice in letters, Blair/Orwell promptly moved to Hampstead, the neighborhood in London at the time for hip young writers, and took a job at a used bookstore, which gave him time to write. In rapid succession, he wrote two novels, *Burmese Days* and *A Clergyman's Daughter*, the latter an experimental novel with an unreliable narrator (she has amnesia) and shifting techniques (there's a chapter written as a script), and laced throughout with anticapitalist sentiment.

## Literary Lessons

Orwell would be at home on today's Internet. He more or less created a new kind of writing: deep, serious, detailed essays about otherwise superficial topics. Orwell was like a one-man BuzzFeed, writing about topics like postcards, how to make the perfect cup of tea, and the difference between British and American dime-store novels.

In his thirties, Orwell wrote prolifically on a number of subjects for periodicals, which is how he made ends meet. The most famous was "Shooting an Elephant," a 1936 story about an Englishman (assumed to be Orwell) ordered to shoot an ill-tempered elephant in Burma. He does so, and it eats him up inside. Thematically, shooting the elephant is a metaphor for the English attempting to conquer and stifle the world through imperialism; in the story, the elephant is killed and the narrator is destroyed, implying that imperialism ruins all parties. Orwell says, quite clearly:

> "When the white man turns tyrant, it is his own freedom that he destroys."

The story, and stating its theme, is also indicative of Orwell's attitude toward his audience. His writing was clear and direct, removed of frills and pomp and with tremendous economy of language, similar to his American contemporary Ernest Hemingway. Orwell wanted as wide an audience as possible to read and understand his work, particularly the uneducated and lower classes he was forever interested in liberating.

## AN UNCLEAR FUTURE

Taking his offensive on corruption and unchecked power further, Orwell fought in the Spanish Civil War for the Republicans, where he was shot and almost died. He later joined POUM, a Spanish socialist party that emphasized the working class and opposed the Communists' middle-class collaboration. This left him with a hatred of totalitarianism, especially Stalinism, and inspired Orwell's famous novel, *Nineteen Eighty-Four* (1949). With it, Orwell introduced a new concept in science fiction, and all of literature: the dystopia.

Up until this point, literature had always been striving for a better future, but with *Nineteen Eighty-Four*, Orwell posited *what if it's worse?* His future is the result of imperialism and totalitarianism gone unchecked, a bleak world divided into three equally oppressive nations that use surveillance ("Big Brother is watching") and propaganda to control every aspect of life. To that end, Orwell produced one of the most popular and influential science-fiction novels of all time, and demonstrated that the genre most associated with dime-store novels was capable of deep literary value.

## Quotable Voices

"i. Never use a metaphor, simile, or other figure of speech which you are used to seeing in print.

ii. Never use a long word when a short word will do.

iii. If it is possible to cut out a word, always cut it out.

iv. Use the active rather than passive voice.

v. Never use a foreign phrase, a scientific word, or a jargon word if you can think of an everyday English equivalent.

vi. Break any of these rules sooner than say anything outright barbarous."

—Orwell's six rules of good writing, from "Politics and the English Language"

Like some other disillusioned people of his generation, Orwell believed that totalitarian governments would inevitably take over the West. They didn't, but the "nanny state" of omnipresent surveillance certainly took hold in the UK.

# DOWN ON THE FARM

Orwell's other major novel was *Animal Farm* (1945), an anti-Soviet satire that is set in a seemingly idyllic pastoral setting and centers on two pigs representing Leon Trotsky and Joseph Stalin. A blistering and very topical takedown of Communism ("All animals are equal, but some are more equal than others") and totalitarianism in the power vacuum at the end of World War II, Orwell's book suggests that the people are not to blame as much as the corrupt leaders who will do anything to keep the people down and themselves in power. Largely pessimistic, Orwell writes that humans are unable to govern themselves, and certainly not in a system that's innately corrupt. And he does all of this with talking barnyard animals.

The Widening Definition of "Englishness"

English literature comprises a period of more than 1,000 years. It's a collection of works that is constantly changing and evolving. The rapid growth of literature forced the English language to adapt, too, so its writers could have more tools at their disposal to express themselves and describe the human condition.

This adaptation continues among English writers to this day, who are boldly making sense of the world as it grows ever more complicated. Today's major writers couldn't help but be influenced by the staggering legacy of authors of the past, but they're just like Shakespeare or Austen or Chaucer or Eliot: They've used a marvelous language to tell marvelous, fascinating, and universal stories.

Here's a look at some of the major voices in British literature over the last few decades up through the present day.

## ZADIE SMITH

The Cambridge-educated daughter of an English father and a Jamaican mother, Zadie Smith depicts the ethnically and culturally rich London of the twenty-first century. A literary star before the age of thirty with her novel *White Teeth* (2000) about three diverse and interconnected families, she's also won awards for her novels *NW*, *On Beauty*, and *The Autograph Man*.

# HILARY MANTEL

Hilary Mantel is a major figure in historical fiction, who uses the luxury of historical perspective to make periods and icons of British history come alive for modern-day readers. Her best-known work is a trilogy of novels about the rise and fall of Thomas Cromwell in the court of Henry VIII:

- *Wolf Hall*
- *Bring Up the Bodies*
- *The Mirror and the Light*

Neither dry like a history textbook or a glowingly positive biography, Mantel's depiction of real people from Britain's past shows them how they were: violent, psychologically complex, and human.

# KAZUO ISHIGURO

Kazuo Ishiguro writes in the florid, languid, nature-glorifying style of E.M. Forster or Thomas Hardy, but subverts the style with a modern edge. Ishiguro writes about the Victorian themes of longing and the madness of forced rules, but injects progressiveness, sentiment, and even science fiction. His novels take place in a world similar to this one, but with a few details just slightly off to create a dissonance.

His Booker Prize–winning *The Remains of the Day* takes place in the late 1940s, but a reader could be convinced it takes place in the late Victorian era. Ishiguro's atmospheric novel of young love gone awry, *Never Let Me Go*, is outfitted with a sci-fi twist. He trades in flawed characters, and his books rarely feature any kind of resolution for their characters.

## Literary Lessons

While it's no longer the most commercially successful literary style, English poetry is still vital. The United Kingdom even still appoints an official poet laureate. Major poets to hold the position include Carol Ann Duffy (2009 to the present), Ted Hughes (1984–1998), and Cecil Day-Lewis (1968–1972). Born in Ireland and educated at Oxford, Day-Lewis published a dozen volumes of his own poetry and translated the major works of the Roman poet Virgil into English, as well as published more than twenty popular mystery novels under the pen name Nicholas Blake. Three-time Academy Award–winning actor Daniel Day-Lewis is his son.

# NEIL GAIMAN

Neil Gaiman is nearly a one-man legacy of the British canon. He writes gothic-style horror (*The Graveyard Book, Coraline*) that is enjoyed by children and adults, but he also possesses a droll, cutting British wit (*Good Omens*) worthy of Wilde or Wodehouse. Gaiman came to prominence with his graphic novel series The Sandman (1989), which has been one of the few graphic novels ever to make it on the *New York Times* bestseller list, as well as one of the first comic books to be accepted as legitimate literature.

A number of Gaiman's highly inventive works have also been turned into movies, including his fantasy novel *Stardust* (2007) and *Coraline* (2009), while currently under development are *The Graveyard Book, The Sandman,* and a TV series adaptation of his mythology-inspired novel *American Gods* (2001). His 2013 novel *The Ocean at the End of the Lane*, which is relatively light on the fantastical elements, won the British National Book Award for Book of the Year.

# NICK HORNBY

Nick Hornby is the bard of modern-day British manliness—and laziness. Speaking from the Gen-X perspective, Hornby's characters are white British males who feel lost and misguided by a Thatcher-era system that failed them. Hornby's characters have grown up with him, from the soccer-loving youth in his memoir *Fever Pitch* to the commitment-phobic, music-obsessed record store clerk in *High Fidelity*. Hornby writes about the same pop culture that his characters are obsessed with, since this culture is as universal a religion for twentieth-century Britons as the Church of England was 300 years prior.

# HAROLD PINTER

A Nobel Prize–winning playwright who spoke out about British interference around the globe, Harold Pinter moved from dull drawing-room plays to stark, subtle dramas (*The Birthday Party*) told in real time, or even backward (*Betrayal*'s scenes are presented backward to heighten the tragedy of a dissolving marriage). His realism is palpable, but his characters all share the stiff upper lip of British culture, and are terrified of revealing their true selves. The dialogue in Pinter's plays is almost always short, clipped, and loaded with subtext. For what the Nobel Prize committee called uncovering "the precipice under everyday prattle," in 2005 Pinter joined George Bernard Shaw and Samuel Beckett as the only playwrights from the British Isles to ever win the Nobel Prize for Literature.

# MARTIN AMIS

Martin Amis is the son of comic novelist Kingsley Amis (*Lucky Jim*), and the Oxford graduate published his first novel, *The Rachel Papers*, in 1973, followed quickly by *Dead Babies* and *Success*. He's been one of the most thoughtful English novelists of the last few years alongside contemporaries like Salman Rushdie. His writing straddles the literary/commercial line, similar to authors like John Updike and Saul Bellow, featuring epic tales of regular if exceptional men caught up in the trappings of modern life. His London trilogy—*Money*, *London Fields*, and *The Information*—deals with the greed and corruption of the Thatcher years. He points out the absurdity via over-the-top caricature to bring to light the unpleasantness and cruelty of capitalism and white privilege.

# J.K. ROWLING

With the Harry Potter series, J.K. Rowling reinvented the Tolkien-style, sprawling-universe fantasy novel, but set it in the present day, creating a pop cultural phenomenon never quite seen before. Rowling's tales play on classic themes—good versus evil—but are quintessentially British. After all, the majority of the action takes place in a centuries-old boarding school in which students wear uniforms and are separated into different "houses." The books have universal appeal and made Rowling the first author to earn $1 billion.

But despite its modern setting, the Harry Potter series, of which the first book was published in 1997, already ranks in the English literary canon. That's due in part to how it embraces and depicts classical themes that have been deeply ingrained into English-language readers. Elements of Harry Potter can be traced back to the very first English story. In *Beowulf,* a special individual is selected as the only person who can defeat the great evil threatening the kingdom. And Beowulf does, only to have to take up arms against the dark force once again. The Harry Potter series follows a similar track: Young wizard Harry refuses to die—as a baby—at the hands of the evil wizard Voldemort. Seven books later, Voldemort regroups, amasses an army, and Harry defeats him again with his own troops. There just isn't a theme more universal than good defeats evil.

# Index

*Agnes Grey* (A. Brontë), 146

*Alice* books of Lewis Carroll, 154, 156–58

Amis, Martin, 246

*Animal Farm* (Orwell), 240–41

*An Apology for the Life of Mrs. Shamela Andrews* (Fielding), 92

Arthurian legends (King Arthur), 32–35
  about: overview of, 32
  Caxton, William and, 34–35
  *The Fairie Queene* and, 55
  historical context, 32–34
  Malory, Thomas and, 33–35
  Tennyson and, 129, 131, 132
  Welsh origins, 32–34

Auden, W.H., 207–8

Austen, Jane, 107–9
  other novels by, 107–8, 109
  *Pride and Prejudice* by, 107, 108–9
  *Sense and Sensibility* by, 107, 108

*The Ballad of Reading Gaol* (Wilde), 171

*The Battle of the Books* (Swift), 82–83

Bede, St. (the Venerable Bede), 13–16

*Beowulf*, 17–20
  stories of, 17
  survival and revival of, 20
  time frame/age of, 18–19
  Tolkien and, 20, 232

Bibles, 25–27, 38–42

Blake, William, 115–18
  *Milton* by, 116
  other works by, 117–18
  "The Tyger" by, 117, 118

Blank verse, creation of, 50–51

*The Book of Common Prayer*, 43–45

*The Book of the Order of Chivalry* (Caxton), 34–35

Brontë sisters, 142–47
  *Agnes Grey* by Anne, 146
  death of, 146–47
  *Jane Eyre* by Charlotte, 144–45
  names and pseudonym success, 142, 143–44
  novels by, 144–47
  poems by, 143–44
  settings of works, 142–43
  *Wuthering Heights* by Emily, 145

Browning, Robert and Elizabeth Barrett, 148–53
  "The Cry of the Children" by Elizabeth, 153
  Elizabeth's background and works, 150–53
  *An Essay on Mind, with Other Poems* by Elizabeth, 151
  "Isobel's Child" by Elizabeth, 152
  "Lady Geraldine's Courtship" by Elizabeth, 153
  *Poems* by Elizabeth, 150
  Robert's background and writing style/themes, 148–50
  *The Seraphim, and Other Poems* by Elizabeth, 152

Burns, Robert, 123–26

Byron, Lord, 110–14
  *Childe Harold's Pilgrimage* by, 111, 112
  *Don Juan* by, 112–13
  early publication, 110
  travel, beauty, and writing, 111–12
  writers influencing, 112

*The Canterbury Tales* (Chaucer), 29–31, 34

*Captains Courageous* (Kipling), 166
Carroll, Lewis, 154–58
    *Alice* books of, 154, 156–58
    children's books and poetry by, 157
    entertaining Liddell family children, 155, 157
    real name, pen name, 154, 155
    silly/crazy poems and stories, 155–56, 157–58
    words made up by, 155
Catholic Church
    Bede's writings and, 13
    *The Book of Common Prayer* and, 44–45
    Church of England split from, 22, 25, 38, 39, 201
    Donne, John and, 46–47
    "Glorious Revolution" and, 68
    King James Bible and, 38–40, 41–42
    Pope, Alexander and, 86
    prohibiting English-translation Bible, 27
    Swift satirizing, 83
    Tolkien, J.R.R. and, 231
    *The Vision of Piers Plowman* criticizing, 22, 23
    Wycliffe's Bible and, 25, 27
Caxton, William, 34–35
Charles I, King, 67
Charles II, King, 67
Chaucer, Geoffrey, 28–31
    *Beowulf* and, 20
    *The Canterbury Tales* by, 29–31, 34
    English language establishment and, 28
    introducing heroic couplet, 28–29
    kidnapping of, 28
    stories in poem form, 30–31
*Childe Harold's Pilgrimage* (Byron), 111, 112
Christianity. *See also* Bibles; Catholic Church; Church of England

    *The Book of Common Prayer* and, 43–45
    C.S. Lewis books and, 234–36
    Donne, John and, 46–48
    *Ecclesiastical History of the English People* (Bede) and, 13–16
    *The Vision of Piers Plowman* (Langland) and, 22, 24
*A Christmas Carol* (Dickens), 134, 135–36
*The Chronicles of Narnia* (Lewis), 236
Church of England
    Blake, William and, 116
    *The Book of Common Prayer* of, 43–45
    Defoe pamphlet satirizing, 79
    Donne, John and, 46, 47
    Eliot, George and, 138
    Eliot, T.S., 186
    Jonson, Ben and, 58
    King James Bible and, 38, 39–40, 41–42
    Lewis, C.S. and, 231
    split from Catholic Church, 22, 25, 28, 38, 39
    Swift satirizing, 83
Coleridge, Samuel Taylor
    adding words to English language, 105
    compared to Wordsworth, 104
    "The Eolian Harp" by, 104
    "Kubla Khan" of, 105
    *Lyrical Ballads* by Wordsworth and, 101, 102, 103–4
    reviving Shakespeare interest, 106
    "The Rime of the Ancient Mariner" by, 103, 104
    unfinished projects of, 106
    Wordsworth, William and, 101, 102, 103–4
Conceit, metaphysical, 48–49
Conrad, Joseph, 222–26

existentialists and, 226
immigration from Eastern Europe, 222–23
life at sea, 223
*Lord Jim* and *Heart of Darkness* by, 224, 225–26
writings of, 223–26
Contemporary English literature, 213–47. *See also* Lewis, C.S.; Tolkien, J.R.R.
about: overview of, 212–13
Conrad, Joseph, 222–26
current voices, 242–47
Doyle, Sir Arthur Conan, 214–17
Golding, William, 227–30
Orwell, George, 237–41
Shaw, George Bernard, 218–21
Cranmer, Thomas, 43–45
Cromwell, Oliver, 67, 70
Cromwell, Thomas, 243
"The Cry of the Children" (E. Browning), 153
*Daniel Deronda* (Eliot), 141
Defoe, Daniel, 78–81
popularizing modern novel, 79, 81
*Robinson Crusoe* by, 79–81, 85
*Devotions upon Emergent Occasions* (Donne), 48
Dickens, Charles, 133–36
*A Christmas Carol* by, 134, 135–36
as cultural and literary influence, 134–36
first modern novels by, 133
legacy of, 133, 136
literature from everyday life, 133–34
setting modern novel standards, 133, 134–35
*A Tale of Two Cities* by, 135
Dictionaries, various, 98
*A Dictionary of the English Language* (Johnson), 95–98
Dodgson, Charles. *See* Carroll, Lewis
*Don Juan* (Byron), 112–13

Donne, John, 46–49
*Devotions upon Emergent Occasions* by, 48
early works, 47–48
metaphysical conceit of, 48–49
metaphysical poets and, 48
"Pseudo-Martyr" essay, 47–48
renouncing Catholic faith, 47–48
Doyle, Sir Arthur Conan, 214–17
other works by, 216, 217
Sherlock Holmes character/writings and, 214–15, 216, 217
Watson and, 215
*The White Company* by, 216
*Dubliners* (Joyce), 202–3
"Easter, 1916" (Yeats), 178
*Ecclesiastical History of the English People* (Bede), 13–16
*Eclogues* (Pope), 87
Eliot, George, 137–41
*Daniel Deronda* by, 141
expanding viewpoint, 140–41
*Middlemarch* by, 140, 141
*The Mill* by, 139
realism of, 138–39
real name of, 137
*Romola* by, 140–41
*Silas Marner* by, 139
starting out as female writer, 137
on top literary concepts, 137–38
Eliot, T.S., 181–86
American expat writers and, 182
"Gerontion" by, 184
inspiration for *Cats* musical, 185
"The Love Song of J. Alfred Prufrock," 182, 183
other works by, 185–86
*Poems* by, 183–84
Pound, Ezra and, 182
"The Wasteland" by, 184–85
Elizabethan era, 36–66
about: overview of, 36–37

*The Book of Common Prayer*, 43–45
Donne, John and, 46–49
Jonson, Ben, 58–61
King James Bible, 38–42
Marlowe, Christopher, 50–53
Shakespeare, William, 62–66
Spenser, Edmund, 54–57
Empiricism, 73, 76, 150
English literature, overview of, 9–10
"The Eolian Harp" (Coleridge), 104
*An Essay Concerning Human Understanding* (Locke), 75–76
*An Essay on Criticism* (Pope), 87, 89
*An Essay on Mind, with Other Poems* (E. Browning), 151
*Every Man in His Humour* (Jonson), 59
*The Fairie Queene* (Spenser), 54–57
*Far from the Maddening Crowd* (Hardy), 173–74
Faustus, *The Tragical History of the Life and Death of Doctor Faustus* and, 50–52
Fielding, Henry, 90–93
    *An Apology for the Life of Mrs. Shamela Andrews* by, 92
    frivolous plays by, 91
    *The History of Tom Jones, a Foundling* by, 90, 93
    *Pamela* parodies of, 91–92
    pseudonym of, 91
    satirical prose of, 91–93
*Finnegan's Wake* (Joyce), 206
Forster, E.M., 192–96
    *Howard's End* by, 194
    Italy and, 192–94
    *The Longest Journey* by, 193
    *A Passage to India* by, 195
    *A Room with a View* by, 194
    *Where Angels Fear to Tread* by, 193
    world wars, philosophy and, 195–96
*Frankenstein* (Shelley), 122

Gaiman, Neil, 244
"Gerontion" (Eliot), 184
Golding, William, 227–30
Gothic romanticism, Walpole, Shelley and, 119–22
Great Bible of 1539, 39
*Gulliver's Travels* (Swift), 84–85
Hallam, Arthur, 129–30
Hardy, Thomas, 172–75
    *Far from the Maddening Crowd* by, 173–74
    other works by, 173, 174–75
*Heart of Darkness* and *Lord Jim* (Conrad), 225–26
Henry VIII, King, 22, 39, 243
Heroic couplets, 28–29, 31, 51, 89, 111
*Historia ecclesiastica gentis Anglorum* (Bede), 13–16
*Historia Regum Britanniae (The History of the Kings of Britain)*, 32, 33
*The History of Tom Jones, a Foundling* (Fielding), 90, 93
*The Hobbit* (Tolkien), 232, 233, 234
Hornby, Nick, 245
Howard, Henry, Earl of Surrey, 66
*Howard's End* (Forster), 194
*Idylls of the King* (Tennyson), 131–32
*The Iliad* (Homer), 58, 89
*The Importance of Being Earnest* (Wilde), 169–70
Irish writers. *See* Joyce, James; Shaw, George Bernard; Swift, Jonathan; Yeats, William Butler
Ishiguro, Kazuo, 243–44
"Isobel's Child" (E. Browning), 152
James, King. *See* King James Bible
James II, King, 73–74
*Jane Eyre* (C. Brontë), 144–45
Johnson, Samuel, 94–98
    biography about, 94
    *A Dictionary of the English Language* by, 95–98

dictionary structure and, 97–98

metaphysical poets and, 48

Jonson, Ben, 58–61

*Every Man in His Humour* by, 59

killing actor in duel, 58–59

*The Masque of Blackness* by, 60

other plays by, 61

Joyce, James, 201–6

*Dubliners* by, 202–3

*Finnegan's Wake* by, 206

legacy of, 206

mastering languages, 201–2

*A Portrait of the Artist as a Young Man* by, 203

*Ulysses* by, 203–6

*Jungle Book* series (Kipling), 165–66

*Kim* (Kipling), 166–67

King Arthur. *See* Arthurian legends (King Arthur)

King James Bible, 38–42

development of, 39–41

as English Bible, 41–42

naming of, 42

other Bibles and, 38–39

printing of, 41

Tyndal's Bible and, 39

Wycliffe's Bible and, 38

Kipling, Rudyard, 164–67

*Captains Courageous* by, 166

*Jungle Book* series by, 165–66

*Kim* by, 166–67

"Kubla Kahn" (Coleridge), 105

*Lady Chatterley's Lover* (Lawrence), 190–91

"Lady Geraldine's Courtship" (E. Browning), 153

*Lady Windermere's Fan* (Wilde), 169

Langland, William, *The Vision of Piers Plowman* by, 21–24

Lawrence, D.H., 187–91

*Lady Chatterley's Lover* by, 190–91

*The Rainbow* and *Women in Love* by, 189–90

*Sons and Lovers* by, 189

*The White Peacock* by, 188

writings on love, sex, relationships, 187, 188–91

*Le Morte d'Arthur* (Caxton), 34, 35

Lewis, C.S., 231, 234–36

Liddell, Henry and family, 155, 156, 157

"Lines Written a Few Miles above Tintern Abbey" (Wordsworth), 102, 104

Locke, John, 73–77

empiricism and, 73, 76

*An Essay Concerning Human Understanding* of, 73, 75–76

issues informing writings of, 73–74

philosophies of, 76–77

*Two Treatises of Government* by, 73, 74–75

worldwide impact of, 76–77

*The Longest Journey* (Forster), 193

*Lord Jim* and *Heart of Darkness* (Conrad), 224, 225–26

*Lord of the Flies* (Golding), 227–30, 236

*The Lord of the Rings* (Tolkien), 20, 232–34

"The Love Song of J. Alfred Prufrock," 182, 183

Luther, Martin, 39

*Lyrical Ballads* (Wordsworth and Coleridge), 101, 102, 103–4

Malory, Thomas, 33–35

Mantel, Hilary, 243

Marlowe, Christopher, 50–53

creating blank verse, 50–51

Faustian bargain with Satan, 51–52

Shakespeare and, 53

*The Tragical History of the Life and Death of Doctor Faustus* by, 50–52

*The Masque of Blackness* (Jonson), 60

Metaphysical conceit, 48–49

Metaphysical poets, 48. *See also* Donne, John

*Middlemarch* (Eliot), 140, 141

*The Mill* (Eliot), 139

*Milton* (Blake), 116

Milton, John, 69–72
  *Paradise Lost* of, 70–72
  selling publishing rights cheap, 72

Modernist movement, 176–211
  about: overview of, 176
  Auden, W.H., 207–8
  Eliot, T.S., 181–86
  Forster, E.M., 192–96
  Joyce, James, 201–6
  Lawrence, D.H., 187–91
  Thomas, Dylan, 209–11
  Woolf, Virginia, 197–200
  Yeats, William Butler, 177–80

"A Modest Proposal" (Swift), 83

Monsters, Gothic romanticism and, 119–22

Motte, Benjamin, 85

*My Fair Lady* (Shaw), 220

*Nineteen Eighty-Four* (Orwell), 239–40

"Nineteen Hundred and Nineteen" (Yeats), 177, 178

Novel, origins of, 79, 81

*The Odyssey* (Homer), 58, 89, 205

Old English literature, 11–35. *See also* Arthurian legends (King Arthur); Chaucer, Geoffrey
  about: first English book, 13–16; overview of, 11–12
  *Beowulf*, 17–20
  *Historia ecclesiastica gentis Anglorum* (Bede), 13–16
  *The Vision of Piers Plowman* (Langland), 21–24
  Wycliffe's Bible, 25–27

*Old Possum's Book of Practical Cats* (Eliot), 185

Orwell, George, 237–41

*Animal Farm* by, 240–41
  "classless" experiment, 237–38
  *Nineteen Eighty-Four* by, 239–40
  other works by, 238–39

*Out of the Silent Planet* (Lewis), 235

*Paradise Lost* (Milton), 70–72

*A Passage to India* (Forster), 195

*Pastorals* (Pope), 86–87

*The Picture of Dorian Gray* (Wilde), 170

Pinter, Harold, 245–46

Poems. *See also specific poems; specific poets*
  ballade style, 56
  blank verse origin, 50–51
  earliest. *See Beowulf; The Vision of Piers Plowman*
  epic *The Rape of the Lock* by, 87–89
  heroic couplets, 28–29, 31, 51, 89, 111
  iambic pentameter, 51, 55, 63, 66, 89
  iambic trimeter, 51
  longest, 17
  metaphysical poets and, 48

*Poems* (E. Browning), 150

*Poems* (Eliot), 183–84

*Poems* (Tennyson), 130–31

*Poems Chiefly in the Scottish Dialect* (Burns), 124–25

Pope, Alexander, 86–89
  *Eclogues* by, 87
  emulating classics, 86–87
  *An Essay on Criticism* by, 87, 89
  other works by, 89
  *Pastorals* by, 86–87

*A Portrait of the Artist as a Young Man* (Joyce), 203

*Pride and Prejudice* (Austen), 107, 108–9

"Pseudo-Martyr" essay (Donne), 47–48

*Pygmalion* (Shaw), 219, 220, 221

*The Rainbow* and *Women in Love* (Lawrence), 189–90

Raleigh, Sir Walter, 54

*The Rape of the Lock* (Pope), 87–89

Restoration and beyond, 67–98
    about: overview of, 67–68
    Defoe, Daniel, 78–81
    Fielding, Henry, 90–93
    Johnson, Samuel, 94–98
    Locke, John, 73–77
    Milton, John, 69–72
    Pope, Alexander, 86–89
    Swift, Jonathan, 82–85
"The Rime of the Ancient Mariner"
    (Coleridge), 103, 104
Robinson Crusoe (Defoe), 79–81, 85
Roman Britain and Roman Empire,
    13–16
Roman Catholic Church, 25, 44
Romantic era, 99–126. See also
    Coleridge, Samuel Taylor
    about: overview of, 99–100
    Austen, Jane, 107–9
    Blake, William, 115–18
    Burns, Robert, 123–26
    Byron, Lord, 110–14
    Walpole, Shelley, and Gothic
        romanticism, 119–22
    Wordsworth, William, 101–2
Romola (Eliot), 140–41
A Room of One's Own, 199–200
A Room with a View (Forster), 194
Rowling, J. K., 246–47
The Screwtape Letters, 235–36
Sense and Sensibility (Austen), 107, 108
The Seraphim, and Other Poems (E.
    Browning), 152
Shakespeare, William, 62–66
    Beowulf and, 20
    Coleridge reviving interest in, 106
    Globe Theatre productions, 64–65
    most direct influence on, 53
    plays of, 63–64
    sonnets of, 66
    writing greatness, 62–63
Shaw, George Bernard, 218–21

    My Fair Lady by, 220
    Nobel Prize for Literature, 221
    other works by, 220–21
    Pygmalion by, 219, 220, 221
    theatre influencing, 218–20
Shelley, Mary, 121–22
Shelley, Percy Bysshe, 121, 178
Silas Marner (Eliot), 139
Smith, Zadie, 242
Sonnets, 46, 54, 66
Sons and Lovers (Lawrence), 189
Southey, Robert, 143
Spenser, Edmund, 54–57
    ballade style poems and, 56
    The Fairie Queene by, 54–57
    political writings of, 56–57
    Raleigh, Sir Walter and, 54
    A View of the Present State in
        Ireland by, 57
Stevenson, Robert Louis, 159–63
    other island-inspired books, 163
    Strange Case of Dr. Jekyll and Mr.
        Hyde by, 160, 161–62
    travel-inspired books, 160
    Treasure Island by, 160, 161, 162
    writers influencing, 162
Strange Case of Dr. Jekyll and Mr. Hyde
    (Stevenson), 160, 161–62
Stream of consciousness writing,
    198–99
Surrey, Henry, 51
Swift, Jonathan, 82–85
    "A Modest Proposal" by, 83
    The Battle of the Books by, 82–83
    groundwork for literary satire, 82
    Gulliver's Travels by, 84–85
    A Tale of a Tub by, 83
A Tale of a Tub (Swift), 83
A Tale of Two Cities (Dickens), 135
Tennyson, Alfred Lord, 129–32
    early works, 129–30
    Hallam, Arthur and, 129–30

*Idylls of the King* by, 131–32
*Poems* by, 130–31
"The Princes," views of women and, 132
Thomas, Dylan, 209–11
  celebrity of, 210–11
  *Under Milk Wood* by, 210–11
Time, *anno Domini* (AD) and, 14
Tolkien, J.R.R., 231–36
  *Beowulf* and, 20, 232
  Lewis, C.S. and, 231, 234–36
  life and works, 231–34
*The Tragical History of the Life and Death of Doctor Faustus* (Marlowe), 50–52
*Treasure Island* (Stevenson), 160, 161, 162
*Two Treatises of Government* (Locke), 73, 74–75
"The Tyger" (Blake), 117, 118
Tyndal, William, and Tyndal's Bible, 39
*Ulysses* (Joyce), 203–6
*Under Milk Wood* (Thomas), 210–11
Vaughn, Henry, 48
Victorian era and Industrial Revolution, 127–75
  about: overview of, 127–28
  Brontë sisters, 142–47
  Browning, Robert and Elizabeth Barrett, 148–53
  Carroll, Lewis, 154–58
  Dickens, Charles, 133–36
  Eliot, George, 137–41
  Hardy, Thomas, 172–75
  Kipling, Rudyard, 164–67
  Stevenson, Robert Louis, 159–63
  Tennyson, Alfred Lord, 129–32
  Wilde, Oscar, 168–71
*A View of the Present State in Ireland* (Spenser), 57
*The Vision of Piers Plowman* (Langland), 21–24

alliteration and illustration, 23
Christianity and, 22, 24
Langland and, 21
poetic structures of, 23
visions and symbols, 22
Walpole, Horace, 120–21
"The Wasteland" (Eliot), 184–85
*Where Angels Fear to Tread* (Forster), 193
*The White Company* (Doyle), 216
*The White Peacock* (Lawrence), 188
Wilde, Oscar, 168–71
  *The Ballad of Reading Gaol* by, 171
  gross indecency, homosexuality and prison, 170–71
  *The Importance of Being Earnest* by, 169–70
  *Lady Windermere's Fan* by, 169
  *The Picture of Dorian Gray* by, 170
Woolf, Virginia, 197–200
  *To the Lighthouse* by, 198–99
  *A Room of One's Own* by, 199–200
  stream of consciousness writing, 198–99
Wordsworth, William, 101–2
*Wuthering Heights* (E. Brontë), *145*
Wycliffe, John, and Wycliffe's Bible, 25–27
  challenging established rule and religion, 26–27
  King James Bible and, 38
  Wycliffe's birth and background, 25–26
Yeats, William Butler, 177–80

# ABOUT THE AUTHOR

Brian Boone is an editor and writer for the bestselling Uncle John's Bathroom Reader line of trivia and humor books. He wrote *I Love Rock 'n' Roll (Except When I Hate It)* published by Penguin/Perigee, and coauthored *American Inventions: Big Ideas That Changed Modern Life* (Time-Life) and *How to Make Paper Airplanes* (The Child's World). He has contributed to HowStuffWorks, Barnes & Noble Reads, McSweeney's, Splitsider, Someecards, *The Onion*, ClickHole, Adult Swim, and Funny or Die. He lives in Oregon with his family.